ADA CARTIANU

THE SANITY OF THE OUTCAST

WHY BEING LABELED A "LUNATIC" IS A BADGE OF HONOR IN A SOCIETY SLIDING TOWARDS OPPRESSION, CONTROL AND INDOCTRINATION

THE SANITY OF THE OUTCAST
WHY BEING LABELED A "LUNATIC" IS A BADGE OF HONOR IN A SOCIETY SLIDING TOWARDS OPPRESSION, CONTROL AND INDOCTRINATION

TABLE OF CONTENTS

To the countless unsung heroes—the whistleblowers, the activists, the everyday citizens who have risked everything to speak truth to power, even when branded as "lunatics." Your courage inspires us all, and this book is a testament to your unwavering commitment to justice and freedom. This is dedicated to those who have been silenced, those who have been imprisoned, and those who continue to fight for a more just and equitable world, even in the face of overwhelming odds.

Their sacrifices should never be forgotten, and their fight must be carried forward by each and every one of us who cherish our freedoms. May this work serve as a small tribute to your enduring legacy and a call to action for future generations. Your courage is a beacon of hope, illuminating the path toward a brighter future.

PREFACE

For years, I've witnessed with panic and disbelief the insidious crawl of authoritarianism in a society that represents the standard of true democracy. Alarmed by the future consequences, I've seen the slow, methodical erosion of democratic values. It's a process often cloaked in the language of order, nationalism and stability, but underneath lies the chilling reality of suppressed voices, curtailed freedoms, and the gradual dismantling of the very institutions that protect us. Being born in a former Communist country ruled by a Dictator, I've seen firsthand the devastating effects of silencing dissent, the way in which those who dare to challenge the established order are marginalized, ridiculed, and even persecuted. This book is not just an academic analysis; it's a passionate plea, born from years of analyzing the crises in political systems and from my personal experience in the fight for freedom. It's a reflection on the crucial role of dissent in a healthy society, and a stark warning about the dangers of complacency in the face of rising authoritarianism. It is my hope that this work will serve not only as a chronicle of the challenges we face but also as a powerful call to action, urging readers to engage in the fight for justice, equality and a society where the voices of the outsiders are not just heard, but respected and heeded. It is a challenge to all to stay vigilant, to speak out, and to actively participate in preserving the delicate balance of freedom that defines a truly democratic society. The true fight is just at the beginning, and each one of us has a role to play.

INTRODUCTION

"The Sanity of the Outcast" is a journey into the heart of dissent, an exploration of the courage it takes to challenge power, and the vital role it plays in preserving democracy. This book is not for the faint of heart. It delves into the uncomfortable truths about the dangerous ways in which authoritarianism takes root, often subtly, gradually eroding freedoms until it's too late. It examines how those who dare to speak truth to power are often labeled as "lunatics," "radicals," or "enemies of the state." Through a blend of historical analysis and contemporary examples, this book reveals the patterns of authoritarianism, showcasing how seemingly minor restrictions on speech and assembly can accumulate to drastically limit individual liberties. We will analyze the psychological mechanisms that allow populations to gradually accept limitations on their liberties, and the ethical implications of remaining silent in the face of injustice. This book is a call to unite, a plea for vigilance, and a celebration of the indomitable human spirit that refuses to be silenced. It is a reminder that our freedoms are not guaranteed, that they must be fiercely protected and actively defended. The narratives of activism contained within these pages are a testament to the power of resistance and the enduring hope for a more just and equitable world. The fight for freedom is a constant battle, one that requires courage, resilience and an unwavering commitment to the principles of democracy. It is my sincere hope that this book will inspire readers to become active participants in shaping a more just and democratic future.

THE CRACKS IN THE MIRROR

A CALL TO "LUNACY"
IN AN AGE OF DECEPTION

We live in a precarious age, one where the siren song of conformity threatens to drown out the vital whispers of individual conscience. The comfort of fitting in, of adhering to the perceived "norm," is a powerful lure. But what happens when that "norm" is a carefully constructed facade, a veneer of stability masking a slow, insidious descent into authoritarianism? What happens when the very institutions designed to protect us become complicit in silencing dissent and eroding our fundamental rights? Then, the act of questioning, of refusing to blindly follow, becomes not just an act of defiance, but an act of sanity.

The political situation we live these days paints a stark picture of such a world, an environment where the cracks in the mirror of our shared reality are widening. It is a world increasingly dominated by forms of populism and concentrated power, where in some regions oligarchs manipulate political agendas, and certain censors slide into our digital lives disguised as benevolent safety measures. In this climate, to challenge the status quo, to point out the flaws in the system, is to risk being labeled a "lunatic," a paranoiac, or simply "difficult." Yet, embracing this very label might be the most responsible and morally imperative path one can take.

The danger of conforming to a deceptive norm lies in its inherent capacity to normalize injustice. When dissent is demonized, critical thinking is stifled, and genuine dialogue is replaced with echo chambers of pre-packaged narratives. The comfortable silence of complicity becomes deafening, drowning out the voices of the marginalized and allowing the erosion of rights to proceed unchecked. This is a world where the truth becomes a casualty of power, and individual liberties are sacrificed at the altar of perceived security.

In such a context, the individual conscience becomes a vital bulwark against the tide of oppression. To resist the pressure to conform, to dare to question the narrative being presented, requires courage and a willingness to stand alone. It means acknowledging the dissonance, the uncomfortable feeling that something is fundamentally wrong, and refusing to ignore it for the sake of social acceptance. It means recognizing the cracks in the mirror, the distortions and manipulations that threaten to fracture our understanding of reality.

Embracing the label of "lunatic" in the pursuit of justice is not merely a matter of individual defiance; it is an act of solidarity. By refusing to be silenced, by speaking truth to power, we create space for others to do the same. We break the spell of conformity and empower others to recognize and resist the oppressive forces at play. We remind ourselves and those around us that there is strength in numbers, and that even the smallest voice can contribute to a chorus of resistance.

In this book I am calling for a re-evaluation of what constitutes sanity in an age of deception. Is it truly sane to blindly accept the status quo, to ignore the warning signs of encroaching authoritarianism for the sake of comfort and convenience? Or is it more sane to embrace the discomfort of dissent, to risk the label of "lunatic" in the pursuit of a more just and equitable world? The answer lies in recognizing the cracks in the mirror and daring to challenge the distorted reflection they present. It lies in remembering that the individual conscience, even in the face of overwhelming societal pressure, remains a powerful force for change, a lighthouse of hope in a world desperately in need of light.

The Anatomy *of a* Dying Democracy

A PHILOSOPHICAL AND POLITICAL SCIENCE AUTOPSY

Democracy, once hailed as the pinnacle of political organization, is facing an unprecedented crisis of legitimacy and function. While its formal structures remain intact in many nations, the underlying principles and practices that sustain it are demonstrably eroding. This essay will perform an autopsy on a dying democracy, employing both philosophical and political science lenses to diagnose the causes of its decay and explore the potential for its revival, or the grim reality of its ultimate demise.

Philosophically, the death of a democracy often stems from a gradual corruption of its core values. Enlightenment ideals of reason, individual liberty, and equality underpin the democratic project. However, these ideals are susceptible to distortion and manipulation. The rise of relativism, where objective truth is questioned, allows for the proliferation of misinformation and the erosion of trust in institutions. This "epistemic crisis," as some call it, weakens the ability of citizens to engage in informed debate and hold power accountable, a cornerstone of democratic governance. Furthermore, the increasing emphasis on individual rights, divorced from a corresponding sense of civic duty and collective responsibility, can lead to a fragmented society where the common good is sacrificed at the altar of self-interest. This atomization undermines the social cohesion necessary for a thriving democracy. The erosion of shared values, coupled with the rise of identity politics, further exacerbates this fragmentation. When individuals primarily identify with narrow, self-defined groups, the sense of national unity and shared purpose that binds a democracy together can fray, leaving it vulnerable to internal divisions and external manipulation. The philosophical underpinnings of democracy, once a source of strength, become a point of weakness, exploited by those seeking to undermine the system.

Political science offers a complementary framework for understanding democratic decline. Polarization, often fueled by social media algorithms and partisan media outlets, creates echo chambers where opposing viewpoints are demonized and compromise becomes impossible. This gridlock paralyzes government, rendering it unable to address pressing social and economic issues. The rise of populism, driven by anxieties over economic insecurity, globalization, and cultural change, further exacerbates these divisions. Populist leaders, often charismatic and adept at exploiting societal grievances, promise simple solutions to complex problems, often circumventing established democratic norms and institutions in the process. This can manifest in attacks on the judiciary, suppression of dissenting voices, and the manipulation of electoral processes. The careful balance of power, a cornerstone of democratic governance, is disrupted as populist leaders consolidate authority and weaken checks and balances. Furthermore, the professionalization of politics and the increasing influence of money in campaigns contribute to a sense of disconnect between elected officials and the citizens they are supposed to represent. This disconnect fuels cynicism and apathy, further eroding popular support for democratic institutions. The political landscape becomes a battleground for competing factions, each vying for power at the expense of the common good.

Another key factor contributing to democratic decay is economic inequality. As wealth becomes increasingly concentrated in the hands of a few, the political influence of the wealthy elite grows disproportionately. This can lead to policies that favor the rich at the expense of the majority, further exacerbating economic disparities and fueling resentment. The erosion of the middle class, traditionally a bulwark of democratic stability, weakens the social fabric and creates fertile ground for political extremism. This economic marginalization can also lead to disengagement from the political process, as citizens feel that their voices are not heard and that their elected officials are unresponsive to their needs. The promise of equal opportunity, a cornerstone of the democratic ideal, becomes a hollow shell, fostering a sense of injustice and fueling social unrest. The concentration of economic power translates into political power, creating a system where the voices of ordinary citizens are drowned out by the clamor of special interests.

The role of external actors should also not be overlooked. Authoritarian regimes often actively seek to undermine democracies through disinformation campaigns, cyberattacks, and support for extremist groups. This external interference weakens democratic institutions and erodes public trust in democratic processes. The rise of global interconnectedness, while offering many benefits, also creates new vulnerabilities that authoritarian actors can exploit to destabilize democratic societies. The spread of propaganda and misinformation through social media platforms can sow discord and undermine public confidence in democratic institutions. Furthermore, foreign interference in elections can undermine the legitimacy of democratic outcomes and erode public trust in the electoral process. The defense of democracy requires vigilance and resilience in the face of these external threats.

The symptoms of a dying democracy are readily identifiable. Declining voter turnout, particularly among younger generations, signals a growing disillusionment with the political process. Increasing levels of political violence and polarization indicate a breakdown in social cohesion. The erosion of press freedom and the spread of misinformation undermine the ability of citizens to engage in informed debate. The concentration of power in the hands of a few, whether through political manipulation or economic dominance, weakens the checks and balances that are essential for a healthy democracy. The rise of conspiracy theories and the rejection of scientific consensus further erode the foundation of rational discourse and evidence-based decision-making. These symptoms are warning signs that the democratic body is weakening and requires immediate attention.

The prognosis for a dying democracy is grim, but not necessarily terminal. Revitalization requires a multi-faceted approach. Firstly, it demands a renewed commitment to civic education, fostering critical thinking skills and promoting a deeper understanding of democratic principles and values. This includes teaching media literacy to combat misinformation and promoting respectful dialogue across ideological divides. Secondly, it necessitates reforms to address economic inequality, ensuring that the benefits of economic growth are shared more equitably. This may involve progressive taxation, investment in education and job training, and strengthening social safety nets. Thirdly, it requires strengthening democratic institutions, protecting them from corruption and ensuring their accountability. This includes campaign finance reform, stricter ethics rules for elected officials, and independent oversight of government agencies. Fourthly, it demands a robust defense against external interference, protecting the integrity of electoral processes and combating disinformation. This requires investing in cybersecurity, strengthening intelligence agencies, and working with international partners to counter foreign interference. Furthermore, fostering a culture of civic engagement and promoting the participation of marginalized groups are essential steps in revitalizing a dying democracy.

However, even with these efforts, the survival of a democracy is not guaranteed. The forces of decay are powerful and deeply entrenched. The rise of authoritarianism around the world suggests that the democratic project is facing a formidable challenge. The spread of disinformation, the erosion of trust in institutions, and the rise of populism are all symptoms of a deeper malaise. The question is whether democratic societies have the will and the capacity to address these challenges and revitalize their institutions. The ultimate fate of any dying democracy hinges on the willingness of its citizens to actively engage in its revival, to defend its core values, and to hold their leaders accountable. This requires a collective commitment to the principles of democracy, a willingness to compromise, and a belief in the possibility of a better future. If this commitment is lacking, the autopsy will ultimately conclude with a verdict of irretrievable loss. The death of a democracy is not a sudden event but a slow and agonizing process, a gradual erosion of its core values and institutions. It is a tragedy that can be averted, but only through vigilance, courage, and an unwavering commitment to the principles of self-governance. The future of democracy depends on the choices we make today.

The Oligarch's Grip

WHEN WEALTH BECOMES RULE

Democracy, in its purest form, promises a level playing field where every citizen's voice carries equal weight in shaping the collective destiny. However, this ideal often collides with the stark realities of wealth inequality, leading to a phenomenon where economic power subtly, and sometimes not so subtly, morphs into political dominance. This essay argues that when wealth becomes concentrated in the hands of a few, an "oligarch's grip" tightens on the political process, distorting democratic principles, eroding social justice, and ultimately undermining the very foundation of a just society.

The sinister nature of oligarchic control lies in its multifaceted manifestations. Campaign finance laws, often riddled with loopholes, become vehicles for the wealthy to amplify their voices, drowning out the concerns of ordinary citizens. Massive donations translate into access and influence, effectively buying the ears of elected officials. Lobbying, another channel for special interests, allows corporations and wealthy individuals to shape legislation to their advantage, often at the expense of public welfare. Furthermore, the concentration of media ownership in the hands of a few can lead to biased reporting and the suppression of dissenting voices, shaping public discourse in ways that benefit the elite. Even seemingly neutral institutions like "think tanks" can be used to promote policies that align with oligarchic interests, cloaked in the guise of objective research. These mechanisms, often operating in the shadows, create a system where the wealthy few have a disproportionate ability to mold the political landscape to their liking. The result is a subtle but pervasive shift in power away from the people and towards a select group of economic elites.

The consequences of this undue influence are far-reaching and corrosive to the democratic fabric. Policies are increasingly tailored to benefit the wealthy, leading to regressive taxation, deregulation that favors corporations, and the dismantling of social safety nets. This, in turn, exacerbates inequality, creating a society where opportunities are increasingly determined by birthright rather than merit. Public services like education, healthcare, and infrastructure are often underfunded, disproportionately affecting the less fortunate. The result is a vicious cycle where economic inequality fuels political inequality, further solidifying the oligarch's grip. This cycle is self-perpetuating, as the wealthy use their political influence to maintain and expand their economic advantages, making it increasingly difficult for others to climb the economic ladder. The long-term effect is a society divided, where a small elite enjoys immense wealth and power, while the majority struggles to make ends meet.

Examining case studies of countries where wealth has hijacked the democratic process provides stark illustrations of this phenomenon. In some nations, natural resources have been concentrated in the hands of a small elite who wield immense political power, often through corruption and patronage. These "resource curses" demonstrate how the control of valuable resources can lead to the entrenchment of oligarchic power, as the elite use their wealth to maintain their grip on the government and suppress dissent. In others, financial deregulation has allowed the banking sector to dominate the political landscape, leading to policies that prioritize profit over the well-being of the populace. The 2008 financial crisis, for example, highlighted the dangers of unchecked financial power, as banks lobbied for deregulation that ultimately led to a global economic meltdown. These examples demonstrate that the specific mechanisms may vary, but the outcome is the same: a distorted political process that serves the interests of the few at the expense of the many. The rise of populism in many countries can also be seen as a response to the perceived failures of democratic institutions to address the concerns of ordinary citizens in the face of growing wealth inequality.

The erosion of democratic principles under the weight of oligarchy raises fundamental questions about the nature of justice and fairness. Philosophers like John Rawls have argued for a society organized around principles of fairness, where inequalities are only justifiable if they benefit the least advantaged. Oligarchic control directly contradicts this principle, as policies are designed to further concentrate wealth and power at the top, while the needs of the majority are neglected. This ultimately undermines the legitimacy of the political system and breeds resentment and social unrest. When citizens feel that their voices are not being heard and that the system is rigged in favor of the wealthy, they may lose faith in democracy and turn to alternative forms of political expression, some of which may be disruptive or even violent. The erosion of trust in democratic institutions can have profound consequences for social cohesion and political stability.

Combating the oligarch's grip requires a multi-pronged approach that addresses both the symptoms and the underlying causes of wealth inequality and political corruption. Strengthening campaign finance laws to limit the influence of money in politics is crucial. This includes advocating for public financing of elections and stricter regulations on lobbying activities. Transparency in political donations and lobbying efforts is also essential for holding elected officials accountable and preventing corruption. Promoting media diversity and protecting independent journalism are essential for ensuring a vibrant and informed public discourse. This can be achieved through policies that support public broadcasting, promote media ownership diversity, and protect journalists from harassment and intimidation. Furthermore, progressive taxation policies and robust social safety nets are necessary to address wealth inequality and level the playing field. This includes policies such as higher taxes on the wealthy, increased minimum wages, and expanded access to education, healthcare, and affordable housing. Ultimately, education and civic engagement are vital for empowering citizens to recognize and resist the insidious influence of wealth in politics. By educating citizens about their rights and responsibilities, and by encouraging active participation in the political process, we can create a more informed and engaged electorate that is less susceptible to manipulation by wealthy elites.

Moreover, international cooperation is essential to address the global dimensions of oligarchic power. Tax havens and offshore accounts allow the wealthy to evade taxes and hide their assets, further exacerbating inequality. International agreements to combat tax evasion and promote financial transparency are crucial for leveling the playing field and ensuring that the wealthy pay their fair share. Furthermore, international organizations can play a role in promoting good governance and combating corruption in countries where oligarchic power is particularly entrenched.

The concentration of wealth can pose a grave threat to democratic governance, leading to a situation where an oligarch's grip stifles the voices of ordinary citizens and distorts the political process. Understanding the various mechanisms through which this control manifests itself is crucial for developing effective strategies to combat it. By promoting transparency, accountability, and economic justice, we can strive to restore the balance of power and ensure that democracy truly serves the interests of all, not just the wealthy few. The pursuit of a just and equitable society requires a constant vigilance against the insidious influence of wealth and a commitment to upholding the principles of democratic governance. This requires a collective effort from citizens, policymakers, and civil society organizations to challenge the status quo and create a more democratic and equitable society for all. The fight against the oligarch's grip is not just a political battle, but a moral imperative to ensure that democracy lives up to its promise of equal rights and opportunities for all. Only then can we build a society where wealth serves the common good, rather than ruling it.

The Chilling Erosion *of* Freedom

THE SUBTLENESS OF AUTHORITARIANISM

The dangerous nature of authoritarianism lies not in its dramatic coups and overt displays of power, but in its subtle, incremental erosion of freedoms. It is a slow boil, not a sudden explosion, a gradual chipping away at the foundations of liberty until the structure crumbles, leaving its citizens bewildered and unprepared for the stark reality of their subjugation. This process is often so gradual, so seemingly insignificant in its early stages, that it goes largely unnoticed until it's too late. The initial restrictions are presented as necessary measures, temporary inconveniences, or even as improvements to security or social order. This tactic cleverly masks the true intent: to dismantle democratic processes and establish unchecked control.

We can see this pattern repeated throughout history, in nations as diverse as Nazi Germany and the Soviet Union. In Germany, the Weimar Republic's gradual decline wasn't marked by an immediate seizure of power, but rather a series of incremental steps. Initially, relatively minor infringements on civil liberties, justified under the guise of national security or economic stability, were accepted, even by many who would later become victims of the regime. The Enabling Act of 1933, for example, seemingly granted the government temporary emergency powers, yet it paved the way for the dismantling of democratic institutions and the establishment of a totalitarian dictatorship. This was a crucial turning point, but one that came about not through a single, catastrophic event, but through a series of seemingly small concessions.

Similarly, in the Soviet Union, the erosion of freedom began with the suppression of opposition parties and the centralization of power within the Communist Party. Freedom of speech and the press were gradually curtailed, with dissent met with swift and brutal repression. The use of propaganda to manipulate public opinion and instill fear was a key component of this strategy. The Gulag system, while horrific in its ultimate consequences, was not instantaneously implemented. It grew incrementally, starting with arrests and deportations of perceived enemies of the state and slowly escalating to the mass imprisonment and extermination of millions. These seemingly incremental steps—each seemingly justified within a particular political narrative—ultimately led to a state of complete totalitarian control.

The stench of creeping authoritarianism isn't some dusty relic of the past. It chokes the air of our own time, a phantom menace cloaked in the sleek, seductive sheen of sovereignty. Taste the bitter ash of disinformation campaigns, lies so expertly crafted they burn your throat with their deceptive sweetness. The crumbling edifice of trust in institutions; stay lucid and you'll hear the sickening groan of its foundations giving way to a symphony of despair played on shattered ideals. This isn't brute force; this is a slow, agonizing strangulation. Imagine the chilling precision: the ability to manipulate the very information you consume, to shape your perceptions, to turn neighbor against neighbor with a few deft keystrokes. Picture the petrifying quiet of a society where dissent is not silenced with a bullet, but a carefully crafted dogma designed to bury your voice in a cacophony of noise. Feel the icy grip of fear constricting your chest as the regime, unseen, yet omnipresent, exerts its control. The freedom we once took for granted is not shattered by a sledgehammer; it's being meticulously, methodically, "atomized". Each tiny cut, a tiny erosion of hope, bleeds into the next, until we find ourselves shackled not by chains, but by our own silent, self-imposed fear or obedience. The insidious hum of this control is the soundtrack to our potential doom, a lullaby that promises serenity while stealing our very soul.

The silent grip of control. That's what it is. The psychological rope tightens around the minds of the population. I can taste the metallic tang of indoctrination and confusion in the air, the bitter grit of surrender grinding between their teeth. These mechanisms of compliance, these mental contortions… they're not just fascinating, they're terrifying. Cognitive dissonance. An abstract scream muffled by the heavy hand of oppression. It's coming! The dissonance claws at them, a physical ache as they watch their freedoms, one by one, snatched away like prized possessions. Each incremental loss — a disturbing wind whistling through the broken windows of their liberty.

They justify it. They "must".

They twist and turn the narrative, constructing elaborate mental puzzles to rationalize their muddling restrictions and unjustified actions as necessary, sacrifices to the altar of a phantom security, and a false god of stability and sovereignty.

The comfort of the lie is seductive. It's a warm blanket against the icy wind of truth, the truth of a power hungry regime that tightens its grip with every swallowed dissent. It's easier to believe the propaganda, to pretend the gilded cage isn't a cage at all. To believe that the sneaking shadows aren't closing in. But there's something else at play here. Deeper than mere self-preservation. It's the cooling weight of the collective gaze, the fear of isolation that's colder than any winter. At one point, to speak out will mean to risk everything. The distressing whispers of ostracism, the sudden, indifferent silence of former friends, the horrifying efficient shunning - these are weapons more potent than any truncheon. The price of defiance is too steep for many. Silence becomes their refuge, a bitter pill swallowed to maintain a semblance of peace or delusion, even as the rot spreads throughout their very souls. It's a slow, agonizing death of spirit, a surrender to the encroaching night. And that, my friend, that is the true horror.

Another crucial factor is the gradual normalization of oppressive practices. When restrictions are implemented incrementally, each new limitation becomes the new normal, paving the way for further encroachment. What initially might have sparked outrage or protest eventually becomes accepted as routine. This normalization process is aided by government propaganda, which constantly frames these restrictions in a positive light or as necessary evils. The framing often focuses on national security concerns, economic stability, or the fight against some external enemy. This allows the government to present itself as acting in the best interests of its people, while simultaneously undermining their fundamental freedoms.

The erosion of trust in institutions, another key aspect of this subtle process, is crucial to understand. When trust in media, government, and other institutions diminishes, citizens become more susceptible to manipulation and less likely to resist oppressive measures. The spread of disinformation campaigns, often amplified by social media algorithms, further erodes this trust, making it difficult for citizens to distinguish between fact and fiction. This information vacuum allows authoritarian regimes to manipulate public opinion more easily and to discredit any opposition. The combination of a lack of trust in institutions and the flood of disinformation leaves citizens vulnerable to the subtle manipulations of an authoritarian regime.

The chilling effect of potential reprisal also plays a significant role. Even without overt censorship, the mere knowledge that expressing dissent may result in social ostracization, job loss, or legal repercussions can be enough to silence many individuals. This self-censorship prevents the formation of critical mass and ultimately makes it easier for authoritarian regimes to maintain control. The threat of surveillance, even if not always active, acts as a constant reminder that freedom of thought and expression is not absolute. This climate of fear and uncertainty significantly limits the ability of citizens to freely express their views and participate fully in democratic processes.

The gradual shift in power structures can go unnoticed. When an authoritarian leader or party slowly accumulates power, often through legal means and using the existing system against itself, the shift can seem almost imperceptible. This slow consolidation of power, often justified by appeals to tradition, nationalism, or religious values, can gradually transform a democratic society into an authoritarian one, leaving its citizens ill-equipped to resist. The dismantling of checks and balances, the erosion of judicial independence, and the control of the electoral process all contribute to this insidious transformation.

The subtlety of authoritarianism is its most dangerous weapon. The incremental erosion of freedoms, combined with psychological mechanisms that promote conformity and acceptance, allows oppressive regimes to establish control without resorting to dramatic displays of force. Understanding this process, identifying its early warning signs, and fostering a culture of vigilance and active resistance are essential to preserving democratic values and safeguarding the freedoms that are so easily taken for granted. The fight against authoritarianism is not merely a political struggle; it is a constant battle for the very essence of human liberty. The fight, therefore, must be fought not just on the grand stage, but also in the quieter corners, where the seeds of oppression are sown and nurtured.

The Whispers *of* Censorship

SILENCING THE DISSIDENT VOICE

Free speech, the lifeblood of a thriving democracy, allows for the open exchange of ideas, challenges the status quo, and holds power accountable. It is the cornerstone upon which societies built on progress and justice are founded. However, this essential right is facing an insidious threat: the whispers of censorship, subtly and overtly silencing dissident voices and eroding the very foundations of open discourse. From the algorithmic control of information to the demonization of truth-tellers and the weaponization of legal mechanisms, censorship in the modern world is a multi-faceted phenomenon that demands our urgent attention.

One of the most pervasive and often unnoticed forms of modern censorship lies in the algorithmic architecture of social media. While these platforms tout themselves as champions of free expression, their algorithms, designed to maximize engagement, often prioritize sensationalist content over nuanced analysis, creating echo chambers and hindering the dissemination of dissenting viewpoints. Critics are often drowned out by a chorus of carefully curated narratives, effectively silencing their voices even if not explicitly banned. Furthermore, the opaque nature of these algorithms makes it difficult to discern the true extent of their influence, leaving individuals susceptible to subtle forms of manipulation and censorship without even realizing it. This algorithmic bias extends beyond simple content prioritization.

Platforms can quietly shadow-ban users, limiting the reach of their posts without informing them, effectively making their voices disappear from the broader conversation. They can also demonetize content creators who express views deemed controversial, crippling their ability to sustain their work and incentivizing them to self-censor. The lack of transparency regarding these practices makes it exceedingly difficult to hold these platforms accountable for their role in shaping public discourse. The very architecture of the digital public square, therefore, is being subtly re-engineered to favor certain narratives while marginalizing others, all under the guise of neutral algorithms.

Beyond the digital realm, a dangerous trend has emerged: the demonization of journalists and whistleblowers. Those who dare to expose corruption, challenge official narratives, or uncover inconvenient truths are often subjected to smear campaigns, personal attacks, and even legal persecution. By discrediting the messengers, powerful actors seek to discredit the message, effectively silencing uncomfortable truths and discouraging others from coming forward. The erosion of trust in the media and the increasing vulnerability of whistleblowers creates a chilling effect, making investigative journalism and critical analysis increasingly precarious. The attacks on journalists are not limited to online harassment. They often involve coordinated campaigns designed to undermine their credibility, questioning their motives, and even making threats against their safety and the safety of their families. This creates a climate of fear that makes it increasingly difficult for journalists to do their jobs effectively, depriving the public of crucial information and holding powerful interests accountable.

Whistleblowers, who often risk their careers and personal freedom to expose wrongdoing, face even greater challenges. They are often targeted with legal action, subjected to intense scrutiny, and ostracized by their peers. The lack of adequate legal protections for whistleblowers in many countries further discourages individuals from coming forward, allowing corruption and abuses of power to continue unchecked.

Furthermore, the legal system itself is being increasingly utilized as a tool for censorship. Strategic Lawsuits Against Public Participation (SLAPPs), for example, are designed to silence critics through lengthy and expensive legal battles, even when the claims are baseless. These lawsuits are not intended to win on the merits of the case, but rather to intimidate and bankrupt those who dare to speak out. The mere threat of legal action can be enough to deter individuals and organizations from expressing dissenting opinions, effectively silencing them through fear and financial burden. Beyond SLAPPs, governments are also enacting laws that criminalize certain forms of expression, particularly online speech. These laws, often framed as measures to combat hate speech or disinformation, can be used to suppress legitimate criticism of the government or its policies. The ambiguity of these laws allows for selective enforcement, targeting individuals and groups that are perceived as threats to the ruling power. The increasing use of legal mechanisms to stifle dissent poses a serious threat to free speech and undermines the rule of law.

The cumulative effect of these various forms of censorship is the creation of a culture of self-censorship. When individuals fear the consequences of expressing unpopular opinions, they are more likely to remain silent, even when they believe injustice is being done. This chilling effect has a devastating impact on public discourse, stifling creativity, hindering critical thinking, and ultimately undermining the foundations of a democratic society. When fear dictates what we say and believe, we sacrifice our individual autonomy and collectively weaken our ability to hold power accountable. This self-censorship is not always a conscious decision. It can be a subtle and insidious process, where individuals gradually internalize the constraints on free expression and begin to avoid certain topics or viewpoints. This can lead to a homogenization of thought, where dissenting voices are marginalized and critical thinking is suppressed. The long-term consequences of this self-censorship are profound, as it can erode the very foundations of a democratic society and pave the way for authoritarianism.

Moreover, the rise of cancel culture, while often presented as a form of accountability, can also contribute to a climate of censorship. While holding individuals accountable for harmful or offensive behavior is important, the rush to judgment and the disproportionate punishments often meted out in cancel culture can stifle open debate and discourage individuals from expressing unpopular opinions. The fear of being "canceled" can lead to self-censorship and a reluctance to engage in difficult or controversial conversations. It is crucial to distinguish between legitimate accountability and the silencing of dissenting voices through social pressure and intimidation. A healthy democratic society requires a willingness to engage with different viewpoints, even those that are offensive or challenging, and to allow for open and honest debate.

The whispers of censorship are growing louder, threatening to drown out the voices of dissent and erode the very foundation of free speech. By understanding the subtle and not-so-subtle ways in which censorship manifests in the modern world — from algorithmic manipulation and the demonization of truth-tellers to the weaponization of legal mechanisms and the chilling effects of cancel culture — we can begin to resist its insidious influence. Protecting free speech requires vigilance, courage, and a commitment to defending the right of all voices, especially those that challenge the status quo, to be heard. This includes advocating for greater transparency in algorithmic governance, protecting journalists and whistleblowers from harassment and legal persecution, reforming laws that are used to stifle dissent, and fostering a culture of open and respectful dialogue. Only then can we ensure that the cornerstone of our democracy remains strong and that the winds of progress continue to blow freely, carrying with them the diverse and challenging voices that are essential for a healthy and vibrant society. We must actively cultivate a society that values critical thinking, encourages dissent, and protects the rights of all individuals to express their views without fear of reprisal. The future of democracy depends on it.

The Insidious Snake

HOW DEMOCRACIES SLIDE TOWARDS AUTHORITARIANISM

Democracy, often lauded as the pinnacle of political organization, is not an immutable state. It is a fragile ecosystem, constantly susceptible to threats both from within and without. Authoritarianism, its antithesis, rarely storms the gates in a dramatic coup. Instead, it frequently creeps in, a slow and insidious process of democratic backsliding, where freedoms are subtly eroded, institutions are compromised, and the very foundation of self-governance is gradually undermined. Understanding the telltale signs of this "authoritarian creep" is crucial to safeguarding democracy and preventing its descent into tyranny.

One of the most alarming indicators is the erosion of due process and the rule of law. This often manifests in the selective application of justice, where the powerful are shielded from accountability while dissenters are targeted with disproportionate force. Independent judiciaries, once bastions of impartiality, are increasingly politicized, their decisions swayed by executive pressure or legislative manipulation. Legal loopholes are exploited to silence critics and suppress dissenting voices, while due process protections, such as the right to a fair trial and access to legal representation, are curtailed under the guise of national security or public order. The dismantling of due process is not merely a technical matter; it strikes at the very heart of democratic governance, eroding the principle of equality before the law and creating a climate of fear and impunity. This erosion can begin subtly, perhaps with seemingly minor adjustments to procedural rules or the weakening of judicial review powers. Over time, these small changes accumulate, creating a system where the law becomes a tool of control rather than a safeguard of liberty. Furthermore, the deliberate underfunding of legal aid services can disproportionately affect marginalized communities, further exacerbating inequalities and undermining the promise of equal access to justice. The cumulative effect is a system that favors the powerful and silences the vulnerable, a hallmark of authoritarian regimes.

Parallel to this legal decay is the expansion of surveillance powers. Under the justification of combating terrorism or crime, governments amass increasingly intrusive surveillance capabilities. Broadening surveillance laws without proper oversight allows for the indiscriminate monitoring of citizens' activities, both online and offline. Data is collected, analyzed, and potentially used to stifle dissent and control public opinion. In this environment, the very act of expressing unpopular opinions can become a cause for suspicion, leading to self-censorship and a chilling effect on free speech. This constant surveillance creates a society where individuals are hesitant to exercise their fundamental rights for fear of retribution, ultimately undermining the vibrant exchange of ideas essential to a healthy democracy. Modern technology amplifies this threat exponentially. Facial recognition technology, coupled with ubiquitous CCTV cameras, allows for constant tracking of individuals in public spaces. Algorithms can analyze social media posts, identifying potential dissidents and predicting future behavior. The sheer volume of data collected makes effective oversight nearly impossible, creating a system ripe for abuse and manipulation. Whistleblowers who expose these practices often face severe consequences, further discouraging transparency and accountability.

The militarization of law enforcement presents another worrisome symptom. Police forces, traditionally tasked with maintaining public order and protecting citizens, gradually adopt tactics and equipment typically associated with the military. Armored vehicles, assault rifles, and riot gear become standard issue, transforming police officers into enforcers of state power rather than community protectors. This militarization often accompanies a shift in mindset, where the police increasingly view citizens as potential threats rather than individuals entitled to respect and protection. The result is a heightened risk of excessive force, particularly against marginalized communities, and a further erosion of trust between law enforcement and the public. This trend is often fueled by the rhetoric of "war on crime" or "war on drugs," which justifies the use of aggressive tactics and the blurring of lines between military and police functions. The deployment of military-grade equipment in peaceful protests can escalate tensions and lead to violence, further alienating the public and undermining faith in the state's commitment to protecting its citizens. Furthermore, the training and tactics employed by militarized police forces often prioritize control and suppression over de-escalation and community engagement, fostering a climate of fear and distrust.

However, perhaps the most dangerous tool in the arsenal of authoritarianism is the manipulation of public opinion through propaganda and misinformation. This can take various forms, from state-controlled media disseminating biased information to sophisticated online disinformation campaigns designed to sow discord and distrust. Algorithms are weaponized to amplify certain narratives and silence others, creating echo chambers where individuals are only exposed to information that confirms their existing beliefs. Conspiracy theories are cultivated and spread, eroding trust in legitimate sources of information and creating a climate of confusion and paranoia. In this environment, the truth becomes a casualty, and the ability of citizens to make informed decisions is severely compromised. The internet, once hailed as a democratizing force, has become a breeding ground for disinformation, spread rapidly through social media platforms. Foreign governments and malicious actors can easily manipulate public opinion by creating fake accounts, spreading propaganda, and targeting vulnerable populations with personalized disinformation campaigns. The sheer volume and sophistication of these campaigns make them difficult to combat, requiring a multi-faceted approach that includes media literacy education, fact-checking initiatives, and holding social media platforms accountable for the content they host.

Historical examples, from the Weimar Republic to more recent democratic backsliding in countries like Hungary and Turkey, highlight the common threads that bind these processes together. Each case demonstrates how a combination of economic anxieties, political polarization, and weak institutional checks and balances can create fertile ground for authoritarian tendencies to take root. Demagogues exploit these conditions, promising simplistic solutions to complex problems while simultaneously demonizing their opponents and undermining democratic norms. They capitalize on popular discontent, portraying themselves as the only ones capable of restoring order and stability, even if it means sacrificing fundamental freedoms in the process. The Weimar Republic, crippled by economic hardship and political instability, fell prey to the allure of strongman leadership, which promised a return to national glory but ultimately led to the horrors of Nazi Germany. Similarly, in Hungary and Turkey, leaders have systematically weakened independent media, curtailed judicial independence, and suppressed dissent, consolidating power and eroding democratic institutions. These examples serve as stark warnings about the vulnerability of democracies to internal decay and the importance of vigilance in protecting democratic values.

Combating the insidious snake of authoritarianism requires a multi-pronged approach. First and foremost, it demands strengthening democratic institutions and ensuring robust checks and balances on executive power. This includes protecting the independence of the judiciary, safeguarding freedom of the press, and promoting transparency and accountability in government. Secondly, it necessitates fostering a culture of critical thinking and media literacy, empowering citizens to discern truth from falsehood and resist manipulation. This requires investing in education, supporting independent journalism, and promoting open and honest dialogue across ideological divides. Thirdly, it demands addressing the underlying economic and social anxieties that make people vulnerable to demagoguery and authoritarian appeals. This includes promoting economic opportunity, reducing inequality, and strengthening social safety nets. Finally, it requires a global commitment to defending democracy and human rights, holding authoritarian regimes accountable for their actions and supporting democratic movements around the world.

The slide towards authoritarianism is not a sudden cataclysm but a gradual erosion of democratic principles. The erosion of due process, the expansion of surveillance powers, the militarization of law enforcement, and the manipulation of public opinion represent key warning signs that must be recognized and addressed. Vigilance, critical thinking, and a commitment to defending democratic institutions are crucial in preventing the insidious creep of authoritarianism and safeguarding the freedoms that are the foundation of a just and equitable society. Only by actively resisting these incremental encroachments on liberty can we ensure that democracy remains a vibrant and resilient force in the face of these enduring threats. The fight for democracy is not a one-time victory but a continuous struggle, demanding constant vigilance and a steady commitment to the principles of freedom, equality, and justice for all. And that struggle begins with recognizing the subtle ways in which authoritarianism can take root and spread, threatening the very foundations of our self-governance.

The Complicity
of the Crowd

THE SILENCE OF GOOD PEOPLE
IN A DECLINING SOCIETY

The decay of a society isn't always marked by the resounding clash of arms or the blatant pronouncements of tyranny. More often, it unfolds in a quiet, insidious manner, nourished by the silence of the good – the complicity of the crowd. This silence, born from a complex interplay of psychological factors and societal pressures, allows injustice to fester and ultimately undermines the very foundations of a just and equitable world. To understand societal decline, therefore, necessitates a critical examination of why seemingly ordinary, well-intentioned individuals often remain passive observers while wrongdoing unfolds before their eyes. This passivity, however unintentional, acts as a silent endorsement, emboldening the perpetrators and eroding the moral fabric of the community.

The psychology of conformity plays a significant role in this tragic phenomenon. Humans are inherently social creatures, deeply wired to seek acceptance and avoid ostracism. This innate desire to belong makes us susceptible to social pressure, leading us to align our behaviors and beliefs with those of the group, even when those beliefs contradict our own moral compass. Asch's conformity experiments, where individuals knowingly gave incorrect answers to visual perception tasks simply to conform to the majority opinion, vividly illustrate the potent force of this social pressure.

Fear of ridicule, social isolation, and professional repercussions can be powerful deterrents to speaking out, particularly when confronting established power structures or widely held prejudices. This fear is not always irrational; the consequences of dissent can be real and significant, especially for those in vulnerable positions. The need to provide for one's family, protect one's career, or simply maintain one's social standing can create a powerful internal conflict between moral conviction and pragmatic self-preservation.

Adding to this is the sinister fear of ostracism. Historically, dissent has often been met with harsh consequences, ranging from social shunning to outright persecution. This historical baggage continues to haunt the collective consciousness, creating a subconscious fear of being labeled a troublemaker or a traitor. The perceived safety of anonymity within the crowd often outweighs the moral imperative to act, leading individuals to prioritize personal security over collective justice. This fear is often amplified in societies where dissent is actively suppressed or where whistleblowers are penalized, creating a chilling effect that discourages others from speaking truth to power. Furthermore, the rise of social media, while offering a platform for diverse voices, can also exacerbate this fear. The potential for online shaming, doxxing, and targeted harassment can further discourage individuals from expressing dissenting opinions, even when those opinions are grounded in ethical principles. The digital crowd, fueled by anonymity and echo chambers, can be just as oppressive as any historical regime.

Furthermore, cognitive biases play a crucial role in rationalizing inaction. We are adept at constructing narratives that allow us to maintain a positive self-image, even when confronted with our own passivity. The "just-world fallacy," for instance, leads us to believe that people get what they deserve, allowing us to distance ourselves from the suffering of others by attributing it to their own failings. This bias can be particularly dangerous as it allows us to ignore systemic injustices and perpetuate harmful stereotypes. Similarly, the "optimism bias" convinces us that bad things are unlikely to happen to us, making us less likely to intervene on behalf of others who are at risk. This bias can lead to a sense of complacency, where we assume that someone else will take care of the problem, or that the problem will simply resolve itself without our intervention. These biases act as psychological buffers, allowing us to comfortably coexist with injustice without experiencing debilitating guilt or cognitive dissonance. We become masters of self-deception, cleverly justifying our inaction in ways that preserve our sense of self-worth.

The "bystander effect" further exacerbates this problem. This phenomenon, famously illustrated by the Kitty Genovese murder, demonstrates that the presence of others can actually decrease the likelihood of an individual intervening in an emergency. This occurs because of a diffusion of responsibility - each person assumes that someone else will take action, leading to a collective inaction. The more people present, the less individual responsibility each person feels. This effect is particularly potent in situations where the situation is ambiguous or when the roles of victim and perpetrator are unclear. Uncertainty clouds judgment and creates hesitation, delaying or preventing intervention altogether. The ambiguity provides an excuse for inaction, allowing individuals to rationalize their passivity by claiming they were unsure of what was happening or how to respond.

Beyond these psychological factors, systemic issues often contribute to the complicity of the crowd. A lack of accessible information, a biased media landscape, or a culture of deference to authority can all hinder individuals' ability to recognize and respond to injustice. When information is controlled or manipulated, it becomes difficult for individuals to form informed opinions and challenge the status quo. A media landscape that prioritizes sensationalism over substance can further obscure the truth, distracting the public from important issues and reinforcing existing power structures. A culture of deference to authority can discourage critical thinking and independent action, leading individuals to blindly accept the pronouncements of those in power, even when those pronouncements are unjust or harmful.

Overcoming these psychological barriers requires a conscious and proactive effort. We must cultivate a heightened awareness of our own cognitive biases and actively challenge the assumptions that underpin our inaction. Education plays a crucial role in fostering critical thinking and promoting empathy, enabling us to recognize injustice and understand its consequences. Furthermore, creating a culture that values dissent and protects whistleblowers is essential to encouraging individuals to speak out without fear of reprisal. This requires establishing legal protections for whistleblowers, creating safe spaces for dialogue and debate, and promoting a culture of respect for diverse perspectives. Education should also focus on developing media literacy skills, enabling individuals to critically evaluate information and resist manipulation.

Ultimately, the antidote to the complicity of the crowd lies in cultivating individual courage. This requires not just intellectual understanding, but also a conscious commitment to acting in accordance with our moral principles, even when it is difficult or unpopular. We must learn to value integrity over conformity, and to recognize that silence in the face of injustice is itself an act of complicity. This courage is not merely a matter of grand gestures or heroic acts; it is also about the small, everyday choices we make — the willingness to speak up when we witness discrimination, the courage to challenge harmful stereotypes, the commitment to supporting those who are marginalized. By fostering a society where individuals are empowered to speak out, challenge the status quo, and stand in solidarity with those who are marginalized, we can begin to dismantle the silent machinery of societal decline and build a more just and equitable world. The responsibility to break the silence rests with each of us; only through collective action, fueled by individual courage, can we hope to create a society worthy of the name. We must remember that the arc of the moral universe, while long, bends towards justice only because people are willing to bend it.

THE PRICE OF SILENCE
Complicity in Injustice

The insidious snake of authoritarianism, as we've explored, is often masked by a veneer of normalcy. The gradual erosion of freedoms, the subtle shifts in power dynamics, the normalization of oppressive practices—all these contribute to a climate where dissent is stifled, not through brute force, but through the chilling effect of silence. This brings us to a crucial point: the price of silence. It's a price paid not only by those directly oppressed but by the entire society, for the acquiescence of the many empowers the tyranny of the few.

The ethical dimension of silence in the face of injustice cannot be overstated. To stand idly by while fundamental human rights are violated is to become complicit, however inadvertently. This complicity isn't always a conscious act; it can stem from fear, apathy, or a misguided belief that one's individual action can make no difference. However, the cumulative effect of countless individual silences can be devastating. History is replete with examples of how the silence of the majority allowed atrocities to unfold.

Consider the Holocaust. While the Nazi regime's actions were undeniably horrific, the complicity of many Germans, who either actively participated or passively stood by, cannot be ignored. The normalization of antisemitism, the gradual erosion of Jewish rights, the escalation of violence—all these occurred within a society where many remained silent, either through fear, indifference, or a belief that challenging the regime was futile. This silence not only allowed the atrocities to occur but emboldened the perpetrators, fueling the escalation of their brutality. The widespread failure to speak out, to resist, to challenge the rising tide of oppression created an environment where such unimaginable horrors became possible.

The Rwandan genocide offers another stark example of the devastating consequences of silence. The systematic slaughter of hundreds of thousands of Tutsis and moderate Hutus unfolded amidst a backdrop of pervasive silence. While some individuals bravely resisted, the majority remained paralyzed by fear, uncertainty, or a fatalistic acceptance of the unfolding tragedy. The silence of the international community also played a crucial role, failing to intervene effectively despite clear warnings of the impending genocide. The lack of decisive action, the lack of vocal condemnation, the lack of collective outrage—all this contributed to the scale of the devastation.

These historical examples are not isolated incidents; they highlight a recurring pattern throughout history. From the Armenian genocide to the Cambodian Killing Fields, the common thread is the insidious role of silence in allowing oppressive regimes to flourish. The failure to challenge injustice, the reluctance to speak truth to power, the preference for self-preservation over moral responsibility—all these contribute to the creation of an environment where atrocities become possible, and where the victims are abandoned to their fate.

The argument that individual action makes no difference is a dangerous fallacy. While one voice might seem insignificant in the face of overwhelming power, the collective power of many voices can be immense. The courage of a single individual to speak out can inspire others to follow suit, creating a wave of resistance that can challenge even the most oppressive regimes. History is full of examples of seemingly insignificant acts of resistance that, in the aggregate, proved pivotal in challenging tyrannical rule. The whispers of dissent can become a roar, capable of dismantling the foundations of even the most entrenched power structures.

The ethical imperative to speak out, even when it carries personal risks, is critical. The cost of silence is always higher than the cost of speaking out, for silence validates oppression and perpetuates injustice. The fear of retribution, the risk of social ostracism, the potential for personal hardship — these are all valid concerns, but they should not outweigh the moral obligation to defend fundamental human rights and challenge those who would violate them. This is not to suggest reckless actions, but calculated resistance, strategically employed to maximize impact while minimizing unnecessary risk.

The choice between silence and resistance is not a neutral one. It is a moral choice, a choice that carries profound consequences for the individual, the community, and the world. To choose silence is to endorse injustice, to become complicit in the suffering of others. To choose resistance is to embrace the values of freedom, justice, and human dignity, even if it requires confronting fear, hardship, and uncertainty.

In our increasingly interconnected world, the potential for collective action is amplified exponentially. The rise of social media and other digital platforms has created new avenues for dissent, allowing individuals to connect, organize, and challenge power structures in ways that were previously unimaginable. These tools, however, are not without their pitfalls. They can also be manipulated by authoritarian regimes to monitor dissent and control information flows. Nevertheless, the potential for mobilizing collective action remains significant, and the responsibility of utilizing these tools for good outweighs the inherent risks.

We must understand that the price of silence is measured not only in the immediate suffering of those oppressed but also in the erosion of democratic values, the weakening of social fabric, and the enduring legacy of injustice. The courage to speak out, to resist, to challenge the prevailing narrative – these are not mere acts of defiance; they are acts of moral responsibility, acts that safeguard the very foundations of a just and equitable society. To remain silent is to be a silent accomplice in the slow, insidious erosion of the very freedoms we hold dear. The fight for freedom is a collective endeavor, and the absence of a single voice weakens the chorus of resistance. Choosing to speak is not just a choice; it's an imperative. It is the only path towards a future where justice prevails and the price of silence is not paid in the currency of human suffering.

THE POWER OF DISSENT
Voices in Resistance

The chilling effect of silence, as we've discussed, isn't merely a passive phenomenon; it's a deliberate strategy employed by authoritarian regimes to maintain control. But the history of resistance demonstrates that silence is never absolute. Even under the most oppressive conditions, voices of dissent emerge, often in unexpected ways, challenging the dominant narrative and inspiring others to join the struggle for freedom.

Consider the courageous individuals who, during the apartheid era in South Africa, defied the regime's brutal laws. From the defiance campaigns led by figures like Nelson Mandela to the countless acts of individual courage by ordinary citizens, the resistance movement demonstrated the power of collective action in the face of overwhelming oppression. The songs of freedom, the clandestine meetings, the underground networks of support— these were not mere gestures of defiance; they were vital acts of resistance that gradually chipped away at the foundations of apartheid. The power of their dissent, though met with imprisonment, torture, and even death, ultimately played a pivotal role in dismantling the system and ushering in an era of democratic change. Their stories serve as a powerful reminder that even in the darkest of times, the human spirit cannot be entirely extinguished.

The struggle for civil rights in the United States provides another compelling example of the power of dissent. The courageous activists who fought against racial segregation and discrimination employed various forms of resistance, from peaceful marches and sit-ins to more confrontational tactics. The bravery of individuals like Martin Luther King Jr., Rosa Parks, and countless others who endured police brutality, imprisonment, and social ostracism, serves as a testament to the power of unwavering conviction. Their actions, often met with intense hostility and violence, eventually led to landmark legislation that transformed American society, demonstrating that persistent and organized dissent can overcome seemingly insurmountable obstacles. Their methods, while diverse, were united by a deep commitment to justice and equality.

The rise of the Solidarity movement in Poland during the Cold War offers a compelling illustration of how dissent can challenge even the most entrenched totalitarian regimes. Led by Lech Wałęsa, the movement leveraged the power of organized labor to challenge the communist government's authority. Their strategies involved strategic use of strikes, boycotts, and underground networks to communicate and organize. The sheer scale of the movement's participation, coupled with its commitment to non-violent resistance, proved crucial in bringing about a peaceful transition to democracy. The movement's success was not guaranteed; it required meticulous planning, unwavering commitment, and a willingness to face significant personal risks. Their narrative serves as a powerful counter-narrative to the notion that resistance is futile against powerful, oppressive regimes.

However, dissent is not always organized or overtly political. Sometimes it's expressed through art, literature, music, or other forms of cultural expression. Throughout history, artists, writers, and musicians have used their creativity to challenge the status quo, expose injustice, and inspire social change. Their work often serves as a powerful catalyst for change, awakening the conscience of the public and prompting dialogue on critical social issues. Consider the powerful anti-war literature of the Vietnam era, the poignant songs of protest that resonated with generations, or the thought-provoking artworks that challenged societal norms. These forms of expression often served as a crucial vehicle for dissent, providing a safe space for expressing dissent and mobilizing collective action, particularly for marginalized groups who had little other recourse to challenge the systems of oppression.

The internet and social media have fundamentally altered the landscape of dissent. While these technologies can be used for surveillance and control, they have also empowered activists and dissidents in unprecedented ways. The Arab Spring uprisings, for example, demonstrated the power of social media in mobilizing mass protests and challenging authoritarian regimes. The ease of information sharing, the ability to organize across geographical boundaries, and the potential for bypassing state-controlled media have given rise to new forms of resistance. Yet, it's crucial to acknowledge the challenges and risks associated with online activism. Governments and powerful entities often employ sophisticated methods to monitor and suppress online dissent, highlighting the need for careful consideration of digital security and the potential for manipulation.

Analyzing successful resistance movements reveals several key strategies: First, the importance of building broad-based coalitions is crucial. Successful movements often bring together individuals and groups from diverse backgrounds, united by a common goal. Second, strategic non-violent resistance is often more effective than violent confrontation. Non-violent resistance can garner broader public sympathy, making it more difficult for authoritarian regimes to suppress dissent. Third, the ability to effectively communicate the movement's message is crucial. This involves crafting powerful narratives that resonate with the public and expose the injustices being perpetrated. Finally, maintaining organizational discipline and internal cohesion is essential for the long-term success of any resistance movement.

The power of dissent, then, lies not just in the ability to challenge authority but in the capacity to inspire collective action, build solidarity, and ultimately, transform societies. It is a testament to the enduring human spirit and a constant reminder that even the most oppressive systems can be challenged and ultimately overcome through the courage of those who refuse to remain silent. The fight for freedom is a continuous struggle, one that demands vigilance, courage, and unwavering commitment to the principles of justice, equality, and human dignity. The voices of resistance, though often marginalized and suppressed, ultimately hold the power to shape the course of history, reminding us that the price of silence is far greater than any risk associated with speaking truth to power. The legacy of those who dared to speak, to act, to resist, will continue to inspire future generations to challenge injustice and fight for a more just and equitable world.

Their stories are not just historical accounts; they are a living testament to the enduring power of dissent.

THE TOOLS OF OPPRESSION, CONTROL AND MANIPULATION

The insidious erosion of freedom isn't solely achieved through brute force; it's a meticulously crafted process, often invisible yet profoundly effective. Authoritarian regimes, whether overtly dictatorial or cloaked in the guise of democracy, utilize a sophisticated arsenal of tools to suppress dissent, control information, and manipulate their populations. Understanding these methods is crucial to recognizing and combating the subtle yet powerful forces that chip away at the foundations of liberty.

One of the most pervasive tools of oppression is propaganda. This isn't simply the dissemination of biased information; it's a sophisticated psychological operation designed to shape public perception, often through subtle manipulation and the repetition of carefully crafted messages. Propaganda relies on appealing to emotions rather than reason, exploiting pre-existing prejudices and fears to create a climate of fear and distrust. Classic examples abound: the Nazi regime's masterful use of propaganda to demonize Jews and other minority groups, or the Soviet Union's relentless promotion of communist ideology to maintain its grip on power. These historical examples demonstrate the chilling effectiveness of propaganda in creating a monolithic worldview, suppressing critical thinking, and silencing dissent.

Today, propaganda has evolved. The rise of social media and the internet has provided new avenues for its dissemination. Sophisticated algorithms curate news feeds, reinforcing existing biases and limiting exposure to alternative viewpoints. Bots and trolls spread misinformation and disinformation, creating echo chambers where false narratives thrive and critical voices are drowned out. The seemingly innocuous act of liking a post or sharing a meme can contribute to the spread of propaganda, unknowingly amplifying messages that undermine democratic values and sow discord. The challenge lies in discerning truth from falsehood in an increasingly complex and fragmented information landscape. Critical media literacy is no longer a luxury; it's a necessity.

Censorship, the deliberate suppression of information, is another cornerstone of authoritarian control. This can take many forms, from outright bans on books and newspapers to the subtle manipulation of news coverage. In some cases, censorship is overt, with the state actively controlling the media and suppressing dissenting voices. In others, it is more covert, with self-censorship prevailing as individuals and institutions choose to avoid controversial topics for fear of reprisal. The chilling effect of censorship extends beyond the explicit suppression of information; it creates a climate of fear and self-doubt, discouraging open discussion and critical inquiry.

Surveillance technologies play an increasingly important role in the suppression of dissent. From CCTV cameras to sophisticated facial recognition software, governments and corporations are able to monitor the activities of their citizens with unprecedented levels of detail. This constant surveillance creates a climate of fear, inhibiting spontaneous expressions of dissent and chilling the exercise of fundamental freedoms. Data harvesting from social media and other online platforms further enhances this capability, allowing authorities to identify potential dissidents and monitor their online activities. The potential for abuse of this technology is immense, as is the erosion of privacy that accompanies its widespread deployment. The absence of oversight and accountability only exacerbates these concerns.

The manipulation of public opinion goes beyond propaganda and censorship; it encompasses a range of tactics designed to influence public sentiment and shape political outcomes. This can include the use of disinformation campaigns, targeted advertising, and the exploitation of social divisions. The fabrication and dissemination of false stories—disinformation—can undermine public trust in institutions and create uncertainty and confusion. Targeted advertising, utilizing sophisticated data analysis, allows political actors to micro-target specific demographics with tailored messages, reinforcing pre-existing biases and manipulating electoral outcomes. The exploitation of social and ethnic divisions, playing on existing prejudices and grievances, creates an environment of fear and distrust, hindering constructive political discourse and preventing effective collective action.

The role of misinformation and disinformation in undermining democratic institutions cannot be overstated. The spread of false or misleading information, often amplified through social media, can sow discord, polarize public opinion, and erode trust in established institutions. The ease with which false narratives can be created and disseminated poses a significant challenge to democratic societies. Combating this requires a multi-faceted approach, involving media literacy education, fact-checking initiatives, and the development of effective strategies to counter disinformation campaigns. However, this challenge extends beyond just technical solutions. It demands a fundamental re-evaluation of our information ecosystem, fostering critical thinking and a culture of responsible information consumption. The fight against misinformation isn't merely a battle against false narratives; it's a fight for the very integrity of our democratic processes.

Case studies from around the world provide stark illustrations of these oppressive techniques in action. The crackdown on dissent in China, with its extensive surveillance network and strict censorship, serves as a stark reminder of the potential for authoritarian regimes to suppress freedom. The use of propaganda and disinformation in Russia to influence elections and sow discord in Western democracies demonstrates the transnational nature of these threats. Even in countries that are ostensibly democratic, the manipulation of public opinion and the erosion of trust in institutions raise serious concerns about the fragility of democratic values. These examples highlight the need for constant vigilance and a commitment to upholding the principles of free speech, transparency, and accountability.

The fight against these tools of oppression requires a concerted effort on multiple fronts. This includes promoting media literacy, empowering civil society organizations, holding governments and corporations accountable for their actions, and developing effective strategies to counter disinformation campaigns. Furthermore, it necessitates a renewed commitment to the principles of democracy, including freedom of speech, the right to information, and the protection of human rights. Ultimately, defending freedom is not a passive endeavor; it demands constant vigilance, active participation, and a commitment to challenging the forces that seek to undermine our democratic institutions and erode the very foundations of liberty. The price of silence, as history repeatedly demonstrates, is far too high. Only through active engagement and unwavering defense of these principles can we hope to preserve the hard-won freedoms that too often are taken for granted.

THE PSYCHOLOGY OF CONFORMITY AND RESISTANCE

The frightening effectiveness of authoritarian regimes lies not only in their overt displays of power but also in their manipulation of the human psyche. Understanding the psychology of conformity and resistance is crucial to comprehending how freedoms are eroded and how they might be reclaimed. This involves examining the subtle yet powerful forces that shape individual choices, prompting some to passively accept oppression while others bravely defy it.

One of the most significant psychological factors influencing conformity is obedience to authority. The Milgram experiment, a landmark study in social psychology, demonstrated the surprising willingness of individuals to inflict harm on others simply because they were instructed to do so by an authority figure. Participants, believing they were administering increasingly painful electric shocks to a learner, continued to obey even when the learner expressed obvious distress. This experiment highlights the power of perceived authority to override personal conscience and moral judgment, a dynamic readily exploited by authoritarian regimes to ensure compliance. The implications are profound: individuals may readily participate in actions that violate their own moral compass if sanctioned by a perceived legitimate authority. This explains, to a large extent, the willingness of individuals to participate in oppressive systems, even when they privately disagree with the system's actions. The fear of retribution, the desire for social acceptance within the established hierarchy, and the perception of the authority's invulnerability all contribute to this dynamic.

Closely related to obedience to authority is the concept of groupthink. This phenomenon occurs when a group prioritizes consensus and harmony over critical evaluation of information and alternative perspectives. Within such a group, dissenting opinions are suppressed, leading to flawed decision-making and a susceptibility to manipulation by those in power. The desire to maintain group cohesion can override rational thought and individual judgment, resulting in collective actions that would be unthinkable if individuals acted independently. History is replete with examples of groupthink leading to disastrous consequences, from the Bay of Pigs invasion to the Challenger space shuttle disaster. In the context of authoritarian regimes, groupthink contributes to the normalization of oppression and the silencing of dissent. Individuals may conform to the dominant ideology not necessarily because they believe in it, but because expressing dissent would risk social exclusion and ostracism. The pressure to conform is often immense, and the cost of deviation can be significant.

The bystander effect further complicates the dynamics of conformity and resistance. This psychological phenomenon refers to the tendency of individuals to be less likely to intervene in an emergency situation when others are present. The diffusion of responsibility, the belief that someone else will take action, prevents individuals from taking personal responsibility. In the context of political oppression, the bystander effect can lead to widespread inaction in the face of injustice. Individuals may witness human rights abuses or the erosion of fundamental freedoms yet remain passive, rationalizing their inaction by assuming others will intervene or that their individual efforts would be futile. This inaction, born of apathy or a calculated avoidance of personal risk, inadvertently strengthens the hand of oppressors. The cumulative effect of countless bystanders remaining silent creates a climate of permissiveness that allows oppression to flourish. The feeling of powerlessness in the face of overwhelming authority is a significant factor here; the perception that resistance is futile can paralyze individuals and hinder collective action.

However, the psychology of human behavior is not solely defined by conformity. The capacity for resistance, for courageous defiance in the face of oppression, is equally important to understand. Several psychological factors contribute to the willingness of individuals to engage in acts of dissent. A strong moral compass, an unwavering belief in justice and human rights, can empower individuals to overcome the pressures to conform and challenge the status quo. This inner strength, fueled by conviction, provides the necessary resilience to withstand social pressure and potential repercussions.

The presence of supportive social networks plays a crucial role in fostering resistance. When individuals feel supported by like-minded peers, they are more likely to express their dissent and engage in collective action. Shared experiences, mutual encouragement, and a sense of collective purpose can counteract the isolating effects of conformity and empower individuals to overcome their fears. The power of solidarity cannot be overestimated. History offers countless examples of resistance movements fueled by social cohesion and mutual support, where individuals, empowered by their collective strength, bravely challenged seemingly insurmountable odds. The sense of community and shared identity can counteract the isolating effects of dissent, providing emotional support and resilience.

In contrast to the passivity fostered by obedience to authority, groupthink, and the bystander effect, courageous resistance requires a different set of psychological drivers. A strong sense of self-efficacy, the belief in one's own ability to make a difference, is essential. Individuals who believe they can effect change are more likely to engage in acts of dissent, even when faced with significant risks. Similarly, a sense of moral obligation—a belief that one has a responsibility to speak up against injustice—is a powerful motivator. This sense of duty overrides the fear of social ostracism or personal harm. The willingness to take personal risks for the sake of a larger cause stems from this deeply held sense of moral responsibility.

The path to resistance often involves a complex interplay of individual psychology, social dynamics, and political realities. Understanding these factors is vital to building strategies for effective resistance movements and strengthening the resilience of democratic societies. The fight against oppression is not simply a political struggle; it is a battle of wills, a contest between the forces of conformity and the enduring human spirit of resistance. The psychological understanding of these competing forces enables us to appreciate both the insidious nature of authoritarian tactics and the potential for individuals, collectively, to overcome them. The fight for freedom is not just about structures and policies; it is deeply rooted in the human capacity for courage, empathy, and unwavering commitment to justice. This inherent human resilience, when nurtured and empowered, provides a powerful counterweight to the forces of oppression.

HISTORICAL PARALLELS AND LESSONS LEARNED

Ancient Greece

THE BIRTH AND FALL OF DEMOCRACY

The Athenian experiment, often lauded as the cradle of democracy, offers a complex and cautionary tale. While its ideals of citizen participation and rule of law remain aspirational, a closer examination reveals the inherent fragility of even the most lauded democratic systems. The Athenian democracy, flourishing in the 5th century BC, was far from the inclusive ideal often portrayed. Slavery formed a cornerstone of Athenian society, with a significant portion of the population denied even basic human rights, let alone political participation. Women, too, were largely excluded from the political process, their roles confined to the domestic sphere. This inherent inequality undermines the notion of a truly representative democracy, highlighting the selective nature of its application.

The success of Athenian democracy was intricately linked to its relatively small and homogenous population. Direct democracy, where citizens directly participated in decision-making, was feasible due to the manageable size of the Athenian citizenry. This intimate scale facilitated robust debate and direct accountability of elected officials. However, this model proved inherently unsustainable as populations grew and societal complexities increased. The inherent limitations of direct democracy, its vulnerability to manipulation by charismatic orators and the potential for the tyranny of the majority, ultimately contributed to its downfall.

The rise of powerful individuals and factions played a critical role in the erosion of Athenian democracy. While the system provided avenues for citizen participation, ambitious leaders could exploit rhetorical skill and popular sentiment to consolidate power. The Peloponnesian War, a protracted conflict between Athens and Sparta, exacerbated internal divisions and weakened the democratic institutions. The war exposed the limitations of Athenian democracy in the face of external threats, revealing its vulnerability to demagoguery and the suspension of civil liberties in times of crisis. The war's prolonged nature led to increased reliance on military authority, diminishing the power of civilian oversight. In essence, the war served as a pressure cooker, accelerating the existing tensions within the Athenian system, pushing it past the breaking point.

The rise of demagogues further undermined democratic norms. Individuals like Cleon, known for his inflammatory rhetoric and disregard for established procedures, exploited the existing anxieties and frustrations to amass influence. By appealing to popular prejudices and playing on fears of external threats, such figures could circumvent established democratic processes, fostering an environment ripe for authoritarian tendencies. The rise of demagoguery underscores the importance of robust institutional checks and balances in preventing the erosion of democratic norms. Without a system of checks and balances, charismatic individuals could easily manipulate public sentiment and dismantle the pillars of a functioning democracy.

Beyond the internal pressures, external factors also contributed to the decline of Athenian democracy. The prolonged conflict with Sparta demonstrated the inherent vulnerabilities of a democracy when faced with a powerful and determined adversary. The demands of war often necessitate the suspension of civil liberties, centralization of power, and a reduction of political participation. This can lead to a gradual erosion of democratic values, making it difficult to return to the status quo ante even after the immediate crisis subsides. The protracted struggle with Sparta proved detrimental to the political and social fabric of Athens, exposing the inherent limitations of the democracy and paving the way for its eventual collapse.

The Macedonian conquest under Philip II and Alexander the Great marked the final chapter of Athenian democracy. The Macedonian army, superior in military might, overwhelmed the Athenian forces, bringing an end to the Athenian experiment. While this was a military defeat, it also symbolized the failure of Athenian democracy to adapt to a changing geopolitical landscape and to withstand external aggression. The Athenian experience serves as a poignant reminder of how internal vulnerabilities can be exploited by external forces to undermine and eventually destroy democratic systems.

The lessons from ancient Greece remain acutely relevant today. The recurring themes of inequality, demagoguery, and external pressures resonate powerfully in contemporary democratic societies. The fragility of democracy, its susceptibility to manipulation by those seeking power, and its vulnerability to both internal decay and external threats underscore the importance of constant vigilance. The Athenian experiment, while a beacon of democratic ideals, also serves as a cautionary tale, highlighting the necessary conditions for its success and the potential consequences of neglecting those conditions.

Moving beyond Athens, other ancient Greek city-states offer further insights into the complexities of democratic governance. Sparta, for instance, presented a stark contrast to Athens, with its rigid oligarchic system emphasizing military discipline and social hierarchy. While Sparta achieved remarkable military success, its system lacked the dynamism and inclusivity of Athenian democracy, ultimately proving less adaptable to changing circumstances. The Spartan experience underlines the importance of finding a balance between order and freedom, between stability and innovation, in designing and maintaining a thriving democracy.

The rise and fall of various ancient Greek democracies reveal patterns of both success and failure. Factors such as the size and homogeneity of the population, the strength of institutions, and the capacity to manage internal divisions and external threats all played significant roles. Success was often contingent upon a delicate equilibrium between citizen participation, effective governance, and resilience against both internal and external challenges. When this equilibrium was disrupted, democratic systems proved vulnerable to collapse.

Examining the ancient Greek experience, it becomes evident that democracy is not simply a set of rules or institutions but a dynamic process demanding constant attention and engagement from its citizens. The constant struggle to balance individual liberties with collective needs, the inherent tensions between consensus and dissent, and the ongoing challenges posed by powerful interests and external forces require continuous vigilance and active participation. The lessons from ancient Greece are not just historical curiosities but essential guides for navigating the complexities of democratic governance in the contemporary world. The ancient Greek experience underscores the need for a robust civic education, the importance of critical thinking in the face of powerful rhetoric, and the necessity for a deep commitment to the principles of equality, justice, and the rule of law.

The fragility of democracy is not a theoretical abstraction but a recurring historical reality. Ancient Greece provides a potent reminder of this vulnerability. The Athenian experiment, with its remarkable achievements and ultimate downfall, remains a vital case study in understanding the dynamics of democratic success and failure. Its lessons, though centuries old, remain profoundly relevant in the face of contemporary challenges to democratic governance. The need for constant vigilance, the importance of citizen engagement, and the understanding of the intricate interplay between internal and external pressures are all critical for safeguarding democratic values in an increasingly complex and volatile world. The stories of ancient Greek democracies serve as a powerful testament to the enduring human aspiration for self-governance and the enduring fragility of the systems designed to achieve it.

The cyclical nature of democratic rise and fall in ancient Greece highlights the continuous effort required to maintain a functioning democracy. It wasn't a static achievement but a dynamic process constantly vulnerable to internal strife and external pressures. The lessons learned from these ancient societies are not confined to the past, but offer invaluable insight into the contemporary challenges faced by democracies globally. The threat of demagoguery, the erosion of institutional checks and balances, and the pressures of external conflicts all echo across millennia, emphasizing the importance of vigilance and active participation in maintaining democratic values. The inherent inequalities within many ancient Greek democracies serve as a stark reminder that true democracy requires not just procedures, but a fundamental commitment to inclusion and equality for all citizens. Only with such a commitment can the pitfalls of selective application of democratic principles be avoided. The cyclical nature of these societies also highlights the crucial role of adaptability. A rigid adherence to past practices without the capacity for evolution and reform can lead to the eventual obsolescence and decline of even the most well-intentioned democratic system. The history of ancient Greece provides a rich and cautionary tale, emphasizing the need for constant vigilance, engagement, and reform in the pursuit of a truly just and equitable society. Only through understanding the past can we hope to navigate the complexities and challenges of preserving democratic governance in the modern world.

Weimar Republic
THE RISE AND FALL

The Weimar Republic, established in the aftermath of World War I, stands as a stark and cautionary example of a democracy's vulnerability to internal decay. Its brief existence, from 1919 to 1933, offers a chillingly relevant lesson for contemporary societies grappling with the rise of extremism and the erosion of democratic norms. Unlike the ancient Greek city-states, the Weimar Republic faced a unique set of challenges, born from the trauma of war, economic instability, and deep societal divisions. The Treaty of Versailles, imposed on a defeated Germany, was deeply resented, creating fertile ground for nationalist resentment and the propagation of conspiracy theories blaming external forces for the nation's misfortunes. This sense of national humiliation and economic hardship, coupled with the trauma of war, fueled a climate of instability and uncertainty, making the fledgling democracy exceptionally vulnerable to manipulation.

The Weimar Republic's constitution, while innovative for its time, suffered from inherent weaknesses. Proportional representation, intended to ensure fair representation of all political factions, ironically proved to be a significant source of instability. The system frequently produced fragmented coalitions, leading to weak and short-lived governments unable to address the pressing economic and social problems facing the nation. The constant shifting alliances and power struggles created a climate of political uncertainty, eroding public trust in the government's ability to govern effectively. This instability created a vacuum that extremist groups, most notably the Nazis, were more than willing to exploit.

The economic woes of the Weimar Republic were particularly devastating. Hyperinflation in the early 1920s wiped out the savings of millions of Germans, creating widespread economic hardship and social unrest. This economic devastation fostered a climate of desperation and disillusionment, leaving many vulnerable to the allure of extremist ideologies promising radical solutions to the nation's problems. The Great Depression, beginning in 1929, further exacerbated the economic crisis, pushing millions into poverty and unemployment. This created a potent breeding ground for social unrest and made the populace receptive to populist and extremist rhetoric. The inability of successive Weimar governments to effectively address this economic crisis undermined public confidence in the democratic system, ultimately contributing to its demise.

The rise of extremism within the Weimar Republic was a gradual process, marked by the increasing influence of radical right-wing and left-wing groups. The Nazi Party, initially a small fringe movement, capitalized on the nation's widespread discontent and disillusionment, skillfully exploiting the existing social and political divisions. Hitler's charismatic leadership and the Nazi Party's skillfully crafted propaganda effectively tapped into widespread anxieties about national humiliation, economic hardship, and the perceived threat of communism. The Nazis' promises of restoring national pride, economic stability, and order resonated strongly with a populace weary of instability and disillusioned with the existing political system.

The failure of the Weimar Republic to effectively counter the rise of extremism can be attributed to several factors. The government's response to extremist violence was often weak and inconsistent, failing to effectively suppress the increasing acts of intimidation and violence perpetrated by Nazi paramilitary groups. This failure to maintain order and protect its citizens further eroded public confidence in the government's ability to govern effectively. The judiciary, burdened by a backlog of cases and hampered by political influence, struggled to effectively prosecute acts of violence and extremism, further emboldening extremist groups. This lack of effective law enforcement and judicial response allowed extremist groups to operate with impunity, further consolidating their power and undermining the authority of the state.

The role of the military in the Weimar Republic's downfall is also significant. While ostensibly loyal to the Republic, elements within the military harbored strong conservative and anti-democratic sentiments. Some officers saw the rise of Nazism as a necessary evil, a means of restoring order and national strength, even if it meant sacrificing democratic principles. This latent anti-democratic sentiment within the military, coupled with its reluctance to effectively suppress the growing power of the Nazi paramilitary forces, ultimately contributed to the Republic's collapse. The military's failure to act decisively against the Nazis emboldened them and facilitated their rise to power. This highlights a critical weakness in many democratic systems—the potential for the armed forces to be susceptible to influence by extremist ideologies, undermining the very foundations of democracy.

The Reichstag fire in 1933, regardless of the true culprits, served as a pivotal moment in the Weimar Republic's demise. The Nazis, exploiting the fear and uncertainty surrounding the incident, used it to justify the suppression of their political opponents and the suspension of basic civil liberties. The enabling act, passed by the Reichstag shortly thereafter, granted Hitler dictatorial powers, effectively ending the Weimar Republic and ushering in the Nazi regime. This event underscores the fragility of democratic systems in times of crisis and the ease with which fundamental rights can be suspended under the guise of national security. This is a crucial lesson for contemporary societies: the preservation of democratic institutions requires constant vigilance and a resolute defence of civil liberties, even during times of upheaval and uncertainty.

The collapse of the Weimar Republic serves as a stark reminder of the fragility of democratic systems and the insidious nature of political extremism. The confluence of factors—economic hardship, political instability, the rise of extremism, and the failure of democratic institutions to adequately respond—led to the demise of a fledgling democracy. The Weimar Republic's experience underscores the importance of strong institutions, a vigilant citizenry, and a resolute commitment to democratic values in safeguarding democratic governance. The lessons learned from its demise hold profound significance for contemporary societies facing similar challenges, emphasizing the critical need for robust checks and balances, strong leadership, and unwavering dedication to the principles of freedom, justice, and equality. The fragility of democratic systems is not a theoretical concept, but a lived historical reality. The Weimar Republic serves as a stark and enduring warning. It is a reminder that democratic values are not self-perpetuating, but require constant vigilance and active participation from its citizens. Only through understanding the past can we hope to build more resilient democracies capable of withstanding the challenges of the present and the future. The seeds of the Republic's demise were sown in the soil of economic instability, political fragmentation, and widespread societal anxieties. These anxieties, expertly exploited by the Nazi party, led to the unraveling of a system ultimately unable to safeguard itself from the forces of extremism. The Weimar Republic serves as a profound warning to all who cherish democratic governance, underscoring the imperative for continuous vigilance and a deep commitment to the values it embodies. Its failure should not be seen as an exception, but rather a chilling testament to the continuous struggle to preserve democracy against the onslaught of authoritarianism and extremism. The ongoing struggle to preserve democratic values, to resist the allure of easy answers and comforting narratives offered by extremist movements, requires a constant, critical engagement with both history and the present. The Weimar Republic's failure resonates deeply with contemporary challenges, serving as a stark reminder that complacency and the erosion of fundamental principles can have devastating consequences. The fight to preserve democracy is a constant struggle, requiring not only strong institutions, but a population well-versed in history, critical of power, and unwavering in its dedication to freedom and justice.

The Soviet Union
OPPRESSION OF DISSENT

The Soviet Union, a behemoth born from revolution, presents a chilling counterpoint to the Weimar Republic's relatively swift collapse. While the Weimar Republic succumbed to the insidious rise of Nazism within a single generation, the Soviet Union's totalitarian grip endured for over seven decades, a testament to the brutal efficiency of its repressive apparatus. Unlike the Weimar Republic's fragmented political landscape, the Soviet Union under Stalin constructed a monolith of power, meticulously dismantling any potential opposition before it could even take root. This control was achieved not merely through force, but through a sophisticated and insidious system of control that permeated every aspect of Soviet life, leaving an indelible mark on the 20th century and offering stark lessons for the preservation of democratic values.

The cornerstone of Soviet oppression was the pervasive and ubiquitous propaganda machine. Every facet of public life, from education and media to art and literature, was meticulously controlled and manipulated to glorify the communist party and its leadership, while simultaneously demonizing any form of dissent or opposition. The official narrative, relentlessly disseminated through newspapers, radio broadcasts, and state-sponsored cultural events, painted a rosy picture of Soviet society, portraying it as a utopian paradise of equality and progress. This carefully constructed image served to bolster the regime's legitimacy, while simultaneously suppressing any alternative perspectives or critical voices. Dissenting opinions were not simply ignored; they were actively erased, their authors silenced or exiled. Independent thought was deemed a dangerous heresy, a threat to the carefully crafted ideological edifice that underpinned the Soviet system.

This propaganda campaign wasn't merely about presenting a positive spin on reality; it was a sophisticated psychological operation designed to manipulate public opinion and maintain absolute control. Individuals were bombarded with constant messaging reinforcing the party line, gradually eroding their critical thinking skills and creating a climate of pervasive fear and self-censorship. Open criticism of the regime became unthinkable; the consequences were too dire. The ever-present threat of denunciation by neighbors, colleagues, or even family members created an atmosphere of suspicion and mistrust, further stifling dissent. This climate of fear, carefully cultivated and meticulously maintained, proved to be remarkably effective in maintaining the regime's grip on power.

Beyond propaganda, the Soviet regime relied heavily on its vast network of secret police, most notably the NKVD (later the KGB), to suppress dissent and maintain order. These agencies employed a wide range of tactics, from surveillance and intimidation to torture and assassination, to eliminate any perceived threats to the regime. Informants were embedded throughout society, meticulously monitoring the activities and conversations of ordinary citizens, reporting any signs of disloyalty or opposition. Even the most private thoughts and actions were subject to scrutiny, fostering a climate of pervasive fear that effectively paralyzed any meaningful resistance. The NKVD's power extended beyond mere surveillance; it had the authority to arrest, imprison, and execute anyone deemed a threat to the regime, regardless of evidence or due process. This unchecked power allowed the secret police to operate with impunity, suppressing any expression of dissent before it could gain traction.

The gulags, the vast network of forced labor camps scattered across the Soviet Union, stand as a grim monument to the regime's brutality and its systematic suppression of dissent. These camps were not merely prisons; they were instruments of terror designed to crush the spirit and eliminate the physical capacity of any opposition. Millions of individuals, from political dissidents and religious leaders to ethnic minorities and perceived enemies of the state, were sent to these camps, where they faced starvation, disease, and brutal treatment. The conditions in the gulags were designed to break individuals, both physically and psychologically, ensuring their complete submission to the regime's authority. The sheer scale of the gulag system—the unimaginable suffering inflicted on millions—serves as a stark reminder of the inhumanity of totalitarian regimes and their ruthless determination to silence any opposition.

Yet, despite the overwhelming power of the Soviet state, resistance to the regime did exist, although it was often clandestine and carried out at great personal risk. Individuals risked their lives to speak out against the injustice and brutality of the regime, distributing samizdat literature, engaging in underground movements, or simply refusing to conform to the party line. These acts of defiance, often carried out in the face of overwhelming odds, demonstrated the human capacity for courage and resilience even in the darkest of times. Their stories, often obscured by the iron curtain of censorship, remind us of the importance of individual conscience and the enduring human spirit's ability to resist oppression.

The Soviet Union's suppression of dissent serves as a chilling reminder of the dangers of unchecked power. The meticulous and multifaceted approach to control—propaganda, secret police, and forced labor camps—created a system that stifled individuality, suppressed free speech, and crushed any opposition. While the Soviet Union ultimately collapsed, the lessons learned from its history remain profoundly relevant today. The ability of a totalitarian regime to control information, manipulate public opinion, and employ terror to maintain power highlights the fragility of democratic values and the importance of constant vigilance in defending against the insidious creep of authoritarianism. The courage of those who resisted, even in the face of overwhelming odds, serves as an enduring testament to the human spirit's capacity for resistance and the enduring importance of freedom and dissent. The echoes of the gulags and the whispers of samizdat continue to resonate, serving as a stark warning of what happens when the pursuit of power transcends all moral and ethical boundaries. The Soviet experiment serves as a chilling case study in the consequences of unchecked power, reminding us of the constant need to safeguard democratic institutions and defend the rights and freedoms that are too easily taken for granted. The struggle for liberty is an ongoing process, one that requires unwavering vigilance and a resolute commitment to the values that define a free and just society. The legacy of the Soviet Union's brutal suppression of dissent is not merely a historical footnote; it serves as a stark and cautionary tale, a reminder of the ongoing struggle to protect democracy from the insidious threat of authoritarianism.

The Cold War
THE STRUGGLE FOR FREEDOM

The Cold War, a protracted geopolitical struggle between the United States and the Soviet Union, cast a long shadow over the latter half of the 20th century. Far from a simple clash of military might, it was a profound ideological battle, a contest between democracy and communism that played out on a global stage, shaping the destinies of nations and the lives of countless individuals. This ideological struggle wasn't confined to the battlefield; it permeated every aspect of life, influencing cultural trends, artistic expressions, and even the everyday conversations of ordinary citizens. The stakes were impossibly high: the very future of freedom and self-determination hung in the balance.

The Cold War's defining characteristic was its inherent paradox: a period of intense tension and near-constant threat of global annihilation, yet one without a single direct military confrontation between the two superpowers. Instead, the conflict manifested in a series of proxy wars, covert operations, and ideological battles fought across the globe. From Korea to Vietnam, from Afghanistan to Angola, the Cold War's shadow stretched across continents, fueling conflicts that claimed millions of lives and left deep scars on the global landscape. These proxy wars were often brutal and protracted, leaving behind devastated nations and populations scarred by violence and political instability. These conflicts weren't simply battles for territory; they were ideological struggles, battles for the hearts and minds of people caught in the crossfire. Each victory or defeat, each shift in the balance of power, reverberated across the globe, shaping the political landscape and influencing the course of international relations for decades to come.

The struggle for freedom during the Cold War wasn't limited to large-scale conflicts; it was fought on a smaller, more personal scale, within the daily lives of individuals who dared to resist oppression. In the Soviet bloc countries, behind the Iron Curtain, countless individuals risked their lives to challenge the totalitarian regimes that controlled their lives. These courageous dissidents, often operating in clandestine networks, used literature, music, and art to subvert state control, expressing ideas and perspectives suppressed by the official narrative. Samizdat, the underground circulation of forbidden literature, became a powerful symbol of resistance, a testament to the human spirit's unwavering pursuit of freedom of expression. These individuals understood the intimate connection between freedom of speech and a free society, recognizing that the suppression of one invariably leads to the erosion of the other.

The Cold War also fostered an environment of intense espionage and intrigue. The CIA and the KGB, the intelligence agencies of the US and the Soviet Union respectively, engaged in a relentless game of cat and mouse, constantly striving to penetrate each other's secrets and undermine each other's influence. This clandestine war, waged in the shadows, involved covert operations, disinformation campaigns, and attempts to recruit and manipulate individuals within each other's spheres of influence. The lives of those caught in this web of espionage were often filled with danger and uncertainty, as they navigated the treacherous terrain of international intrigue, balancing loyalty and personal safety against the broader ideological battle. These individuals, often operating in the shadows, played a crucial role in shaping the Cold War's narrative, gathering intelligence that informed strategic decisions and influencing the course of the conflict. Their stories often remain untold, obscured by the veil of secrecy surrounding their activities.

The impact of Cold War espionage extended beyond the realm of political maneuvering. It had a profound effect on the cultural landscape, influencing the creation of spy novels, films, and television shows that captivated audiences around the world. These fictional accounts, while often embellished or exaggerated, reflected the real-world anxieties and uncertainties of the era, capturing the public imagination and shaping the public perception of the Cold War. This fascination with espionage helped to amplify the ideological battle, influencing public opinion and shaping attitudes towards the opposing superpowers.

The Cold War's legacy extends far beyond the geopolitical landscape. It profoundly impacted the development of international law and human rights. The Universal Declaration of Human Rights, adopted by the United Nations in 1948, emerged from the ashes of World War II and the growing awareness of the atrocities committed by totalitarian regimes during that conflict. The declaration, in its very conception, served as a direct challenge to the Soviet Union's oppressive communist system. It established a framework for the protection of fundamental human rights and freedoms, offering a beacon of hope to those living under oppressive regimes, even as those very same regimes often flagrantly violated the declaration's principles. This inherent contradiction underscored the hypocrisy at the heart of the Cold War's ideological battle.

The Cold War also fostered the growth of international organizations dedicated to promoting human rights and democracy. These organizations, often operating in challenging environments, provided crucial support to activists and dissidents in countries under communist rule, amplifying their voices and providing a global platform for their struggles. They played a vital role in exposing human rights abuses and advocating for democratic reforms, often facing opposition from both communist and authoritarian regimes alike.

However, the Cold War's legacy is not without its complexities. The emphasis on anti-communism during the period sometimes overshadowed concerns about human rights violations in allied nations. The US's support for authoritarian regimes in the name of containing communism is a contentious aspect of the Cold War's history, raising questions about the true commitment of the superpower to the ideals of freedom and democracy that it ostensibly championed. This inherent contradiction is a persistent challenge in assessing the Cold War's full impact.

Looking back, the Cold War era serves as a potent reminder of the fragility of freedom and the importance of constant vigilance in defending democratic values. The ideological struggle between democracy and communism was not simply a geopolitical battle; it was a moral one, a contest between fundamentally different visions of society and human potential. The stories of those who resisted oppression, those who risked their lives for the ideals of freedom, stand as testaments to the enduring human spirit and the indomitable power of hope, even in the face of seemingly insurmountable odds. Their sacrifices remind us that the fight for freedom is an ongoing battle, one that demands constant vigilance, unwavering commitment, and a profound understanding of the historical forces that shape our world. The lessons learned from the Cold War, from the successes and failures of both sides, remain profoundly relevant in the 21st century, as new challenges to democracy and human rights continue to emerge. The Cold War's echo continues to reverberate, shaping global politics and individual narratives alike. Its legacy serves as a stark reminder of the vital importance of upholding the values of freedom and human dignity in the face of oppression, reminding us of the need for constant and unwavering vigilance in defending the hard-won freedoms we so easily take for granted.

Contemporary Authoritarianism

A GLOBAL PERSPECTIVE

The chilling echoes of the Cold War's ideological struggle resonate powerfully in the 21st century, manifesting not as a bipolar confrontation but as a more diffuse, yet equally dangerous, threat to democratic values worldwide. Contemporary authoritarianism, far from being a relic of the past, has adapted and evolved, employing sophisticated strategies to consolidate power and suppress dissent in ways that often defy easy categorization. The battle for freedom, once waged primarily between two superpowers, now unfolds on multiple fronts, in diverse contexts, and with varying degrees of intensity.

One of the most striking features of contemporary authoritarianism is its chameleon-like ability to adapt to the prevailing political climate. Unlike the monolithic, overtly repressive regimes of the Soviet era, many contemporary authoritarian leaders operate within a façade of democratic legitimacy. They may hold elections, albeit deeply flawed ones, and maintain the outward appearance of a functioning legal system, all while systematically undermining the foundations of a truly free and fair society. This deceptive tactic allows them to circumvent international criticism and maintain a degree of domestic support, even among segments of the population who might otherwise oppose them. The manipulation of electoral processes through gerrymandering, voter suppression, and the control of media narratives are common tools employed to consolidate power and maintain a veneer of democratic legitimacy. This makes the fight against such regimes significantly more challenging, requiring a deeper understanding of the subtle ways in which authoritarianism can infiltrate and dismantle democratic institutions.

Consider, for instance, the rise of populist leaders in various parts of the world. Often charismatic and appealing to the grievances of marginalized populations, these leaders skillfully exploit social divisions and economic anxieties to consolidate their power. They employ nationalist rhetoric, often couched in anti-elite and anti-establishment sentiments, to mobilize support and deflect criticism. The erosion of trust in traditional institutions, including the media and the judiciary, further facilitates their ascent. The spread of disinformation and propaganda through social media exacerbates the problem, creating echo chambers where alternative viewpoints are suppressed and the narratives of authoritarian leaders are amplified. This insidious strategy allows them to bypass traditional channels of information and directly appeal to their target audiences, shaping public opinion and influencing the political landscape to their advantage. The effectiveness of this strategy underscores the vulnerability of democratic societies in the face of carefully orchestrated disinformation campaigns and the manipulation of social media. The sheer scale and sophistication of these campaigns present a formidable challenge to those fighting to preserve democratic values.

Another key characteristic of contemporary authoritarianism is the erosion of the rule of law. Undermining the independence of the judiciary, selectively prosecuting political opponents, and using the legal system as a tool of political repression are all common tactics. The weakening of checks and balances allows authoritarian leaders to act with impunity, silencing dissent and consolidating their power without effective legal challenge. This insidious erosion of the rule of law often begins subtly, with seemingly minor changes to legal procedures or the appointment of judges loyal to the ruling power. Over time, these incremental changes accumulate, creating a system where justice is selectively applied and the rights of citizens are systematically disregarded.

The suppression of freedom of speech and assembly are also hallmarks of contemporary authoritarianism. Independent media outlets are often silenced, journalists are persecuted, and critical voices are marginalized. Peaceful protests are met with excessive force, and the use of surveillance technologies is employed to monitor and intimidate dissidents. This systematic suppression of dissent creates an environment of fear and self-censorship, limiting the space for open debate and political participation. The use of sophisticated surveillance technologies, coupled with the ever-increasing power of data collection and analysis, enables authoritarian regimes to monitor the activities of citizens on an unprecedented scale. This level of surveillance can effectively stifle dissent, deter opposition, and create a chilling effect on the expression of dissenting viewpoints.

Examples: In some countries, we witness the steady dismantling of democratic institutions, from the weakening of independent judiciaries to the manipulation of electoral processes. In others, we see the rise of strongman leaders who consolidate power through a combination of populist appeals, repression, and the erosion of the rule of law. These examples are not confined to any particular region; they span the globe, underscoring the global nature of the threat to democratic values. The manipulation of electoral systems is a commonly observed tactic, with governments employing strategies such as gerrymandering, voter suppression, and the manipulation of voter registration processes to maintain their power. The use of propaganda and disinformation campaigns to sway public opinion and suppress dissent also plays a significant role, often leveraging social media platforms to reach wide audiences.

The erosion of democratic values is not confined to overtly authoritarian regimes. Many countries that are considered democracies are experiencing a gradual erosion of democratic norms and institutions, often fueled by rising populism, political polarization, and the spread of misinformation. This subtle form of democratic backsliding is equally dangerous, as it can lead to a gradual weakening of democratic institutions and the gradual expansion of executive power. The decline of trust in institutions, coupled with the spread of disinformation, can create an environment where extremist ideologies and authoritarian tendencies find fertile ground. This gradual erosion of democratic norms can be as damaging as an outright coup, slowly dismantling the foundations of a free and just society.

The global fight for democracy requires a multi-faceted approach. International organizations must play a crucial role in monitoring human rights abuses, providing support to activists and dissidents, and advocating for democratic reforms. Civil society organizations within individual countries must remain vigilant in defending democratic values and holding their governments accountable. Individuals must engage in informed civic participation, actively combating disinformation and promoting critical thinking. The struggle for freedom is far from over; it is a continuous battle that requires constant vigilance, unwavering commitment, and a profound understanding of the challenges and complexities of the contemporary political landscape. The lessons learned from history, particularly the Cold War's legacy, serve as a potent reminder of the fragility of democratic values and the vital importance of defending them against the ever-evolving forms of authoritarianism that threaten them. The fight for freedom is a global struggle, requiring international cooperation and a commitment to the enduring ideals of democracy, human rights, and the rule of law. The challenges are immense, but the stakes are even higher—the very future of freedom and self-determination hangs in the balance.

THE EROSION
OF TRUTH AND TRUST

THE RISE OF DISINFORMATION
AND PROPAGANDA

The insidious creep of disinformation and propaganda, amplified by the digital age, represents a profound threat to democratic societies. No longer confined to state-controlled media outlets or whispered rumors, falsehoods now spread at an unprecedented velocity, exploiting the very technologies intended to connect and inform. The ease with which manipulated images, fabricated quotes, and outright lies can be disseminated via social media, messaging apps, and even seemingly legitimate news websites, has created a landscape of informational chaos, eroding public trust and fueling political polarization. The algorithms governing these platforms, designed to maximize engagement and user retention, often inadvertently amplify the reach of disinformation, creating echo chambers where falsehoods resonate unchecked, reinforcing existing biases, and creating hostile environments for dissenting voices.

Consider the 2016 US presidential election. The revelation of Russian interference, involving the deployment of sophisticated disinformation campaigns on social media, served as a stark wake-up call. These operations, employing fake accounts, botnets, and targeted advertising, disseminated divisive narratives, spread false information about candidates, and sowed discord within the electorate. The sheer scale and sophistication of this campaign exposed the vulnerabilities of democratic systems to foreign manipulation and highlighted the urgent need for greater scrutiny and regulation of online platforms. This was not merely an isolated incident. Similar tactics have been employed in numerous other elections worldwide, demonstrating a disturbing trend of using digital technologies to undermine democratic processes. The ease with which misleading or false information can be tailored and targeted to specific demographics renders traditional fact-checking methods largely ineffective.

The speed at which disinformation spreads online surpasses the capacity of any traditional fact-checking mechanism. By the time a reputable news organization verifies a false claim, it has often already reached millions, potentially irrevocably influencing public opinion. Moreover, the very act of debunking a falsehood can ironically amplify its reach, as the effort to correct misinformation invariably involves repeating it, inadvertently embedding it further into the public consciousness. This paradox presents a significant challenge for those seeking to combat the spread of disinformation. The challenge is further complicated by the fact that the source of disinformation is frequently obscured, making it difficult to attribute responsibility and hold perpetrators accountable.

The proliferation of "deepfake" technology, capable of creating incredibly realistic but entirely fabricated videos and audio recordings, exacerbates the problem. Deepfakes can be used to convincingly portray political figures saying or doing things they never did, undermining public trust and creating confusion about the truth. The potential for deepfakes to disrupt political campaigns, influence elections, and even incite violence is considerable, highlighting the urgent need for developing effective countermeasures. The sheer potential for creating believable fabrications using readily available technology poses a threat unlike anything witnessed before.

The role of social media algorithms in amplifying disinformation cannot be overstated. Designed to maximize user engagement, these algorithms prioritize content that elicits strong emotional responses, regardless of its veracity. This inherent bias favors sensationalist and emotionally charged narratives, often including misinformation and conspiracy theories, further exacerbating the spread of falsehoods. The algorithms effectively create echo chambers, reinforcing existing biases and limiting exposure to diverse perspectives. Users are increasingly exposed to information that aligns with their pre-existing beliefs, creating an environment where alternative viewpoints are marginalized and critical thinking is stifled. The personalized nature of social media feeds allows for hyper-targeted disinformation campaigns, making it exceedingly difficult for individuals to discern fact from fiction.

The impact of this digital deluge of disinformation extends far beyond elections. It erodes public trust in institutions, including the media, government, and scientific expertise. The constant bombardment of conflicting narratives, coupled with the difficulty of verifying information online, creates a climate of uncertainty and cynicism. This erosion of trust has significant societal consequences, hindering collective action on critical issues such as climate change, public health, and economic inequality. When citizens lose faith in the institutions designed to serve them, they become more susceptible to extremist ideologies and conspiracy theories, further destabilizing societies. The erosion of trust undermines the very foundations of a functioning democracy. The ability to rely on shared factual understandings is essential for a healthy society. The deliberate undermining of this ability is a fundamental attack on democratic processes.

The deliberate manipulation of information isn't a new phenomenon; propaganda has been a tool of political power for centuries. However, the digital age has fundamentally transformed the scale, speed, and reach of disinformation campaigns. Previously, the dissemination of propaganda relied on state-controlled media, carefully crafted speeches, and limited print publications. Today, anyone with an internet connection can potentially reach a global audience, creating a vastly more complex and challenging environment for combating the spread of falsehoods. Moreover, the anonymity afforded by the internet allows perpetrators to operate with impunity, making it extremely difficult to trace the sources of disinformation and hold them accountable. This lack of accountability further emboldens the spread of falsehoods, creating a cycle of misinformation that is increasingly difficult to interrupt.

Examples: Consider the anti-vaccine movement, fueled by the spread of misinformation on social media, resulting in outbreaks of preventable diseases. Or the climate change denial campaigns, funded by vested interests and deliberately spreading doubt about scientific consensus, hindering efforts to address this critical global challenge. Or the spread of conspiracy theories about election fraud, threatening to undermine faith in democratic processes. These examples demonstrate the far-reaching and often devastating impact of disinformation on society. The cost of unchecked misinformation is far-reaching, affecting public health, environmental protection, and the stability of democratic institutions.

Combating the rise of disinformation requires a multifaceted approach. This necessitates improving media literacy education to help individuals critically evaluate the information they encounter online. It requires greater transparency and accountability from social media companies, with stronger mechanisms to detect and remove disinformation campaigns. It requires legislative reforms to enhance regulation and address the legal loopholes that currently enable the spread of falsehoods. It also necessitates support for independent journalism and fact-checking initiatives to counter the avalanche of misinformation that inundates the information landscape. Ultimately, the fight against disinformation is a battle for the very integrity of truth and trust in our democratic institutions, a battle that demands constant vigilance and a collective commitment to defending the principles of accuracy and accountability. The implications of inaction are immense, threatening not only our democratic processes but also our collective well-being. The future of informed citizenry and effective governance depends on our ability to navigate this increasingly complex and challenging information environment.

THE ATTACK ON INDEPENDENT JOURNALISM

The erosion of truth and trust, as detailed in the preceding sections, is inextricably linked to the systematic dismantling of independent journalism. The free press, acting as a vital watchdog, is the cornerstone of a functioning democracy. It holds power accountable, exposes corruption, and informs the public, enabling informed participation in civic life. However, in numerous countries across the globe, we are witnessing a concerted and escalating assault on this fundamental pillar of democratic societies. This assault isn't subtle; it's a calculated strategy employed by authoritarian regimes and powerful interests seeking to control the narrative and suppress dissent.

One of the most insidious tactics used to subdue independent journalism is the weaponization of the legal system. Strategic lawsuits against public participation (SLAPPs) are frequently deployed to silence critical voices. These lawsuits, often frivolous and lacking merit, are designed not to win in court but to financially cripple journalists and media outlets through protracted and costly legal battles. The sheer expense of defending oneself against such lawsuits, even if ultimately successful, can force journalists to abandon their investigations or even shutter their publications entirely. The chilling effect of these SLAPPs is undeniable, discouraging investigative reporting that might expose powerful individuals or institutions. The threat of legal action becomes a powerful tool of censorship, preemptively silencing potential critics before they can even publish their work. This tactic is particularly effective against smaller, independent news organizations that lack the resources to withstand protracted legal battles.

Beyond legal harassment, economic pressure is another potent weapon in the arsenal of those seeking to control information. Governments and corporations can exert significant influence over media outlets through advertising revenue, access to information, and state funding. The withdrawal of advertising revenue can cripple a news organization's financial viability, forcing cutbacks, staff reductions, and ultimately, closure. Similarly, restricting access to government information, a fundamental right for journalists, effectively stifles investigative reporting. The selective release of information, or the deliberate withholding of crucial data, can manipulate the narrative and limit the public's understanding of critical issues. State-controlled media, often lavishly funded and enjoying preferential treatment, further exacerbates the imbalance, creating a skewed information landscape where independent voices are marginalized and drowned out by the dominant, often biased narrative.

Intimidation and harassment are other prevalent methods employed to suppress investigative journalism. Journalists who dare to investigate sensitive topics often face threats of violence, online abuse, and physical attacks. These tactics aim to instill fear and self-censorship, discouraging journalists from pursuing critical investigations. The threat of violence is particularly effective in countries with weak rule of law and limited protection for journalists. In such environments, journalists often face a stark choice: compromise their integrity or risk their safety and well-being. The resulting climate of fear inevitably leads to self-censorship, reducing the diversity of voices and diminishing the public's access to critical information.

The digital age has introduced new and even more sophisticated methods of suppressing independent journalism. The spread of disinformation and propaganda, as discussed earlier, is used to discredit legitimate news sources and sow confusion among the public. Through the coordinated spread of false narratives and fabricated evidence, independent journalists can be portrayed as unreliable, biased, or even part of a conspiracy. This calculated erosion of public trust is a fundamental component in undermining the credibility of the free press. Furthermore, online harassment and targeted cyberattacks, often perpetrated by anonymous actors, can overwhelm journalists with abusive messages, doxing, and attempts to disrupt their work. These attacks are aimed not only at intimidating individual journalists, but also at creating a hostile environment that discourages critical reporting.

The consequences of these attacks on independent journalism are profound and far-reaching. When investigative journalists are silenced, accountability diminishes significantly. Corruption, abuse of power, and human rights violations are often left unchecked, eroding public trust in institutions and exacerbating societal inequalities. The lack of credible information hinders informed decision-making by citizens, weakening the democratic process itself. A society without a free and independent press is a society vulnerable to manipulation and control. The public's ability to discern fact from fiction, to hold those in power accountable, and to engage in meaningful civic participation are all severely compromised when independent journalism is suppressed.

The examples of this assault on independent journalism are tragically abundant. In numerous countries, journalists are imprisoned, exiled, or even assassinated for their work. The Committee to Protect Journalists (CPJ) meticulously documents these instances, highlighting the global threat to press freedom. The sheer number of journalists killed, imprisoned, or forced into exile each year is a stark reminder of the risks faced by those who dare to hold power accountable. These attacks on press freedom are not isolated incidents; they are part of a larger pattern of authoritarian consolidation of power. The suppression of independent journalism is a key strategy employed by regimes seeking to control information, silence dissent, and maintain their grip on power.

The ongoing erosion of journalistic standards and the proliferation of misinformation further exacerbate the challenge. The blurred lines between legitimate news and propaganda, fueled by the ease with which misinformation can be disseminated online, create an information ecosystem where discerning truth from falsehood becomes an increasingly difficult task. The rise of clickbait, sensationalism, and partisan media outlets further contributes to the problem, creating a fragmented and often misleading information landscape. This makes the task of independent journalists even more challenging, as they must constantly combat not only the direct suppression of their work, but also the constant assault on the very notion of truth and objectivity.

Combating this assault on independent journalism requires a multifaceted approach. Strengthening legal protections for journalists, providing them with increased security measures, and supporting independent media outlets are crucial steps. Promoting media literacy and critical thinking skills among the public is equally vital, empowering citizens to discern reliable information from propaganda. International organizations and governments must actively condemn attacks on journalists and hold perpetrators accountable. Furthermore, supporting and amplifying the voices of independent journalists through collaborative platforms and international networks is essential to ensure that their work reaches a wider audience and contributes to a more informed global discourse. The fight to protect independent journalism is a fight for the very foundation of democracy itself. It is a battle that must be fought consistently, vigilantly, and with unwavering commitment to truth and accountability. Only through a concerted global effort can we hope to safeguard this crucial pillar of democratic societies and ensure that the vital work of independent journalists can continue, unhindered and unimpeded. The future of informed citizenry and a just society hinges on our collective ability to uphold and defend the principles of a free and independent press.

The WEAPONIZING Of SOCIAL Media

The erosion of trust and truth extends far beyond the realm of traditional media; it has metastasized into the digital sphere, finding fertile ground in the seemingly boundless expanse of social media. These platforms, initially envisioned as tools for connection and community building, have been weaponized into instruments of manipulation, misinformation, and the suppression of dissent.

The very architecture of these platforms, designed to maximize engagement through algorithms that prioritize sensationalism and outrage, has inadvertently fostered an environment ripe for exploitation.

The spread of misinformation, often referred to as "fake news," has become a defining characteristic of the digital age. Sophisticated disinformation campaigns, often originating from state-sponsored actors or well-funded interest groups, leverage the viral nature of social media to disseminate false narratives and fabricated evidence with remarkable speed and efficiency. These campaigns are meticulously crafted, often targeting specific demographics or exploiting existing societal divisions to maximize their impact. The sheer volume of information circulating online, combined with the inherent difficulty of verifying its authenticity, makes it exceedingly challenging for individuals to discern truth from falsehood. This manufactured uncertainty undermines public trust in legitimate news sources and erodes confidence in established institutions.

One of the most insidious aspects of this phenomenon is the deliberate targeting of vulnerable populations. Elderly individuals, for example, may be particularly susceptible to misinformation campaigns exploiting their anxieties or lack of familiarity with digital technologies. Similarly, marginalized communities, often already facing systemic inequalities, can become targets of hate speech and disinformation campaigns designed to further marginalize and disenfranchise them. The consequences of such manipulation can be severe, leading to increased polarization, social unrest, and even violence.

The amplification effect of social media algorithms further exacerbates the problem. Algorithms designed to maximize engagement often prioritize emotionally charged content, regardless of its veracity. This means that false or misleading information, often presented in a sensational or inflammatory manner, is likely to reach a much wider audience than factual, nuanced reporting. This creates a feedback loop, where the most extreme and divisive content gets the most attention, further reinforcing existing biases and exacerbating polarization. The algorithms, in essence, become unwitting accomplices in the spread of disinformation, amplifying voices that sow discord and undermining the credibility of trustworthy sources.

Beyond the spread of misinformation, social media platforms have become breeding grounds for online harassment and hate speech. The anonymity afforded by the internet, combined with the lack of accountability on many platforms, emboldens individuals to engage in abusive behavior with impunity. Targeted harassment campaigns, often involving coordinated attacks from multiple accounts, can be incredibly damaging to individuals, silencing dissenting voices and creating a climate of fear. Journalists, activists, and politicians who dare to challenge the status quo often find themselves subjected to relentless online abuse, ranging from hateful comments and threats of violence to doxing and swatting. These attacks are not merely unpleasant; they can have a chilling effect on free speech, discouraging individuals from expressing their opinions and participating in public discourse.

The role of social media companies in facilitating or mitigating these issues is a subject of intense debate. While some argue that these companies bear a significant responsibility for the content shared on their platforms, others maintain that they should not be held responsible for the actions of individual users. Regardless of one's position on this matter, it's undeniable that social media companies have the power to significantly influence the online environment. Their algorithms, content moderation policies, and enforcement mechanisms all play a crucial role in shaping the flow of information and the experiences of their users. The failure to effectively address the spread of misinformation, hate speech, and online harassment undermines the integrity of these platforms and contributes to the erosion of public trust.

The weaponization of social media is not limited to the spread of disinformation and online harassment; it also extends to the manipulation of elections and political processes. Coordinated disinformation campaigns, often employing sophisticated techniques such as bot networks and astroturfing, can be used to sway public opinion, influence voter behavior, and undermine democratic institutions. These campaigns often target specific voter demographics or exploit existing social and political divisions to maximize their impact. The ability to quickly spread false or misleading information to a vast audience can have a profound effect on election outcomes, threatening the integrity of democratic processes. Furthermore, the use of social media to incite violence and organize extremist groups poses a serious threat to public safety. The ease with which individuals can connect and coordinate their activities online can facilitate the organization of violent protests, riots, and even acts of terrorism.

Examples of this weaponization are abundant and disturbingly effective. The 2016 US presidential election saw the widespread use of Russian-backed disinformation campaigns on social media to influence voter sentiment and sow discord. Similarly, numerous countries have seen the manipulation of social media to spread propaganda, incite violence, and suppress dissent. These instances are not isolated occurrences; they represent a significant challenge to democratic societies worldwide. The ability to spread misinformation, incite violence, and manipulate public opinion through social media platforms poses a fundamental threat to the stability and integrity of democratic systems.

Addressing this multifaceted problem requires a multi-pronged approach. Social media companies must take greater responsibility for the content shared on their platforms, implementing more robust content moderation policies and investing in technologies to detect and remove harmful content. Governments have a crucial role to play in regulating social media platforms and protecting their citizens from the harmful effects of disinformation and online harassment. However, these regulations must be carefully crafted to avoid stifling free speech and innovation. Educating the public about the dangers of misinformation and promoting media literacy skills are equally crucial. Equipping individuals with the critical thinking skills needed to discern truth from falsehood is essential for navigating the complex and often misleading information environment of the digital age. International cooperation is also vital in tackling the transnational nature of disinformation campaigns. Sharing information, developing best practices, and coordinating efforts across borders are necessary to effectively combat the global spread of misinformation.

Ultimately, the weaponization of social media represents a profound challenge to democratic societies. It undermines public trust, erodes faith in institutions, and facilitates the spread of hate and violence. Addressing this challenge requires a concerted effort from social media companies, governments, civil society organizations, and individuals alike. Only through a collective commitment to truth, accountability, and responsible use of technology can we hope to mitigate the harmful effects of social media manipulation and safeguard the integrity of our democratic institutions. The battle for truth and trust in the digital age is far from over; it requires ongoing vigilance and a steadfast commitment to defending the principles of freedom and democracy.

THE DECLINE OF PUBLIC TRUST IN INSTITUTIONS

The erosion of trust, a creeping malaise that has infected the body politic, finds its most potent expression in the declining faith the public places in its institutions. This isn't a mere matter of opinion polls showing wavering approval ratings; it's a fundamental fracturing of the social contract, a weakening of the very bonds that hold a society together. The consequences are far-reaching, impacting everything from political stability to public health decisions, and ultimately threatening the very fabric of democracy itself.

One of the most significant factors contributing to this decline is the pervasive rise of political polarization. The once-common ground, the shared understanding of basic facts and values, has been replaced by an increasingly tribalistic landscape, where individuals identify primarily with their political tribe and view those belonging to opposing groups with suspicion and hostility. This polarization is amplified by the echo chambers created by social media algorithms, where individuals are primarily exposed to information that confirms their pre-existing beliefs, leading to the reinforcement of biases and the rejection of dissenting viewpoints. The result is an increasingly fragmented society, where rational discourse is replaced by ideological warfare and the pursuit of common goals is hampered by mutual distrust.

This division is often exploited by political actors who actively cultivate divisions within the population. Populist leaders, skilled in the art of demagoguery, frequently employ divisive rhetoric to galvanize support and consolidate power. They often target minority groups or scapegoat specific segments of the population to further solidify their base, creating a climate of fear and resentment. This strategy is not new, but the ability of social media to amplify and disseminate these messages with unprecedented speed and reach makes it far more potent than ever before. This creates a feedback loop where extreme views are amplified, further polarizing the population and exacerbating mistrust in the political system.

The proliferation of conspiracy theories is another significant contributor to the decline in public trust. These theories, often lacking any basis in fact, appeal to people's anxieties and frustrations, offering simple explanations for complex problems and providing a sense of order in a chaotic world. The internet, with its seemingly boundless expanse of information and misinformation, has become a fertile breeding ground for these theories, allowing them to spread rapidly and easily across geographical and cultural boundaries. The lack of rigorous fact-checking and the ease with which fabricated evidence can be created and disseminated contribute to the credibility of these narratives, further undermining public trust in traditional sources of information.

One particularly dangerous aspect of the spread of conspiracy theories is their capacity to undermine confidence in scientific expertise and institutions. The rejection of established scientific consensus on issues such as climate change or vaccination has real-world consequences, leading to public health crises and environmental damage. This rejection is often fueled by a distrust of scientists and institutions perceived as part of the "establishment" or controlled by powerful interests. The deliberate dissemination of disinformation, often backed by well-funded interest groups, contributes to this mistrust, creating a climate where scientific evidence is disregarded or dismissed in favor of unsubstantiated claims.

The erosion of social cohesion is also a significant factor contributing to the decline in public trust. The weakening of community bonds, the decline of civic engagement, and the increasing sense of isolation experienced by many individuals have created a climate of distrust and suspicion. The decline in social capital, the network of relationships and connections that bind people together, erodes the shared sense of identity and purpose that is essential for a cohesive society. This erosion of social trust contributes to a sense of powerlessness and disillusionment, leading to decreased participation in civic life and a greater willingness to accept disinformation.

The implications of declining public trust are profound and far-reaching. A loss of faith in democratic institutions can undermine the legitimacy of government, leading to political instability and even violence. When citizens believe that their political system is corrupt or unresponsive, they are less likely to participate in the democratic process, leading to voter apathy and disengagement. This can create a vacuum, allowing extremist groups to exploit the sense of disillusionment and resentment, leading to further political instability.

The decline in public trust also affects the rule of law. When citizens lose faith in the impartiality and fairness of the justice system, they are less likely to respect and obey its rulings. This can result in an increase in crime and civil unrest, further undermining social order. The erosion of trust also hinders effective governance. When citizens are unwilling to cooperate with government agencies or accept the decisions of elected officials, it becomes more difficult for the government to address social problems and provide essential public services. This leads to a vicious cycle of distrust and ineffective governance, further exacerbating the problem.

Addressing the decline in public trust requires a multi-pronged approach. It involves promoting media literacy, strengthening democratic institutions, fostering social cohesion, and countering the spread of disinformation. The media has a crucial role to play in informing the public and holding powerful actors accountable. However, the media itself faces challenges in maintaining public trust in the face of political polarization and the spread of misinformation. This requires media outlets to adhere to rigorous journalistic standards, prioritize fact-checking, and promote transparency.

Governments also have a responsibility to promote transparency and accountability in their actions. This includes strengthening independent oversight institutions, promoting open government initiatives, and combating corruption. Civil society organizations play a vital role in bridging the gap between citizens and government and promoting civic engagement. They can play a crucial role in fostering social cohesion and countering the spread of disinformation. Individuals also have a responsibility to actively engage in the democratic process, inform themselves about important issues, and critically evaluate the information they receive.

The battle for truth and trust is an ongoing struggle. The challenges are complex and multifaceted. But the rewards for successfully combating the erosion of trust are significant. A society built on a foundation of mutual respect, understanding, and faith in its institutions is a society capable of addressing its challenges and achieving its goals. Without this foundation, the risks are simply too great. The future of democracy itself depends on it.

COMBATING DISINFORMATION STRATEGIES FOR RESILIENCE

Combating the insidious spread of disinformation requires a multifaceted approach, a concerted effort that goes beyond simple fact-checking and delves into the very fabric of how we consume and process information. The battleground is not merely the internet, but the minds of individuals, vulnerable to narratives that prey on anxieties and insecurities. The first line of defense, therefore, is education—not just in schools, but in communities and homes. Media literacy, the ability to critically analyze information sources and identify biases, needs to be a fundamental skill, taught as early as elementary school. This isn't about indoctrination; it's about empowering citizens to become discerning consumers of information, capable of identifying credible sources from unreliable ones. The curriculum should include practical exercises, encouraging students to deconstruct news articles, analyze visual media, and recognize manipulative techniques often employed in disinformation campaigns. This education must extend beyond formal schooling, reaching adults through community workshops, online resources, and public service announcements.

The digital age presents both a challenge and an opportunity. While the internet has democratized information, it has also become the primary vector for disinformation campaigns. This necessitates a broader engagement with technology. Social media platforms, often complicit in the spread of false narratives through their algorithms, need to be held accountable. Regulations are necessary, but they must be carefully crafted to avoid stifling free speech while addressing the problem of unchecked dissemination of harmful content. This requires a collaborative approach, involving legislators, policymakers, and technology companies themselves. Independent fact-checking organizations also play a vital role. Their work, however, needs to be amplified and made more accessible to the public. This can involve partnerships with social media platforms to flag false information, the development of easily accessible fact-checking websites and apps, and the integration of fact-checking into educational curricula.

The fight against disinformation cannot be won solely through technological solutions. It requires a renewed focus on fostering critical thinking skills. This involves encouraging individuals to question information sources, assess evidence, and engage in constructive dialogue, even with those who hold opposing views. It requires overcoming the tribalism that plagues our societies, a tribalism exacerbated by the echo chambers created by social media algorithms. Encouraging exposure to diverse perspectives is crucial, promoting open dialogue and fostering a culture of healthy debate. This requires not only individual efforts but also institutional support. Schools, universities, and community organizations need to create spaces for critical discussion, promoting intellectual curiosity and encouraging the exploration of different viewpoints. The media has a crucial role to play here too. Journalism needs to reclaim its ethical grounding, prioritizing accuracy and accountability. This means rigorous fact-checking, transparency in sourcing, and a commitment to presenting a balanced and nuanced portrayal of events.

Moreover, the fight against disinformation necessitates a focus on emotional intelligence. Disinformation campaigns often target vulnerabilities, exploiting anxieties, fears, and prejudices to spread false narratives. Understanding these emotional triggers is crucial in developing strategies to combat disinformation effectively. Educational initiatives can be designed to equip individuals with the skills to recognize and manage their own emotions, fostering resilience against manipulative tactics. This includes teaching critical media literacy, but also understanding the psychology of persuasion and propaganda, helping individuals to identify emotional manipulation within the messaging. The goal isn't to make people impervious to emotion, but rather to equip them with the tools to navigate complex emotional responses in the face of persuasive but potentially deceptive messaging.

Combating disinformation also requires tackling the root causes of its appeal. Often, people turn to conspiracy theories and false narratives because they feel disenfranchised, marginalized, or ignored by the mainstream. Addressing these underlying societal issues is therefore crucial. This involves fostering social cohesion, strengthening communities, and promoting inclusive policies that ensure everyone feels a sense of belonging and participation. This could include investing in community programs, addressing systemic inequalities, and promoting civic engagement. When people feel heard and valued, they are less likely to be drawn to narratives that offer simplistic explanations for complex problems. Political polarization also fuels the spread of disinformation. When society is sharply divided along ideological lines, it becomes easier to spread false narratives that appeal to pre-existing biases and beliefs. Bridging this divide requires a commitment to respectful dialogue, a willingness to engage with those who hold different perspectives, and a recognition that common ground is still possible.

Furthermore, the role of governments and international organizations in combating disinformation is undeniable. Governments need to fund initiatives supporting fact-checking organizations, media literacy programs, and research into the psychology of disinformation. International cooperation is vital, sharing best practices and coordinating efforts to address the transnational nature of disinformation campaigns. The development of robust legal frameworks that address the spread of disinformation without compromising freedom of expression remains a complex challenge, demanding careful consideration of human rights and democratic principles. Striking the right balance is paramount, avoiding overly restrictive measures that could stifle legitimate dissent and create a climate of fear. The legal frameworks need to focus on holding those responsible for the deliberate creation and dissemination of disinformation accountable while protecting the freedom of speech.

The fight against disinformation is not just about identifying and correcting false narratives. It's also about building resilience—the ability to withstand and recover from the psychological and social effects of exposure to disinformation. This includes fostering critical thinking skills, cultivating emotional intelligence, and strengthening social connections. Resilience is built through education, community engagement, and a shared commitment to truth and accuracy. It is a process, not a destination. The fight against disinformation is an ongoing battle, requiring constant vigilance, adaptation, and a commitment to democratic values. It requires a collective effort, involving individuals, organizations, and governments, working together to create a more informed, resilient, and informed society. The stakes are high—the very future of democracy depends on it. The erosion of truth is not merely an abstract concept; it is a tangible threat that undermines the foundations of our societies and necessitates a coordinated and multifaceted response. The fight for truth requires constant vigilance, proactive education, and the unwavering commitment to critical thinking.

The Role of Technology in Authoritarianism

SURVEILLANCE AND THE EROSION OF PRIVACY

This unchecked expansion of surveillance chills dissent, fostering self-censorship and hindering open dialogue crucial for a healthy democracy. Citizens become hesitant to express unpopular opinions, fearing repercussions. The potential for misuse, from targeted harassment to political manipulation, is immense, demanding robust legal frameworks and ethical guidelines. Data breaches further exacerbate these concerns, exposing sensitive personal information. This pervasive monitoring subtly shifts power dynamics, potentially leading to a future where individual freedoms are significantly curtailed. The fight for privacy is thus a fight for democracy itself, requiring vigilance and proactive measures.

The rise of facial recognition technology, for instance, showcases the chilling potential of this trend. Initially touted as a tool to improve public safety, its deployment has expanded far beyond its purported limitations. From tracking individuals' movements in public spaces to identifying protesters at demonstrations, the technology's capabilities far exceed its original application. This expansion has been accompanied by a disturbing lack of transparency and accountability, often bypassing necessary legislative oversight and judicial review. The potential for misuse is staggering; imagine a world where dissent is immediately identified and suppressed, where individuals are preemptively profiled based on algorithms and predetermined biases. This isn't a dystopian fantasy; it is the grim reality shaping the landscape of many nations.

The lack of robust legal frameworks to regulate facial recognition technology is particularly alarming. Many countries have failed to grapple with the complex ethical and privacy implications, resulting in a regulatory vacuum that allows for its unchecked deployment. The absence of meaningful oversight empowers both state actors and private entities to utilize this powerful technology without adequate constraints, creating a landscape ripe for abuse and manipulation. This lack of regulation also fosters an environment of distrust, as citizens are left to wonder about the extent to which their movements and actions are being monitored and analyzed. The chilling effect on free speech and assembly is undeniable, as individuals may self-censor their behavior for fear of surveillance and potential repercussions.

Data mining, another powerful surveillance tool, further exacerbates the erosion of privacy. The seemingly innocuous collection of vast amounts of data from various sources – online activity, social media interactions, purchasing habits, location data – allows for the creation of detailed profiles of individuals. This data is then used not only for targeted advertising, but increasingly for predictive policing and social scoring systems. Predictive policing, based on algorithms that attempt to anticipate future criminal activity, often reinforces existing biases and disproportionately targets marginalized communities. Social scoring systems, prevalent in some authoritarian states, utilize aggregated data to assign individuals a "social credit" score, impacting their access to services and opportunities. This system rewards conformity and punishes dissent, creating a climate of fear and self-censorship.

The implications of these technologies are far-reaching and deeply troubling. The ability to predict and preempt dissent, to identify and suppress opposition before it even manifests, represents a fundamental threat to democratic values. The creation of a surveillance state, where every action is monitored and every individual is potentially profiled, undermines the very principles of freedom and autonomy. The insidious nature of these technologies is that they erode our liberties gradually, subtly, making it difficult to recognize the extent of the damage until it is too late.

Furthermore, the interconnectedness of these technologies compounds their power. The fusion of facial recognition, data mining, and predictive policing creates a sophisticated surveillance apparatus capable of anticipating, tracking, and suppressing dissent with an efficiency that would have been unimaginable just a few decades ago. This interconnectedness also raises concerns about the potential for data breaches and misuse. The sheer volume of personal data collected and stored creates an attractive target for hackers and malicious actors, posing a significant risk to individuals' privacy and security.

Beyond the government, the private sector plays an equally significant role in the pervasive surveillance landscape. Corporations collect vast amounts of data on consumers, often without their informed consent or knowledge. This data is then used for targeted advertising, but increasingly also for other purposes, including profiling and predictive analysis. The lack of transparency and accountability in the private sector's data collection practices further exacerbates the erosion of privacy and raises concerns about the potential for misuse. The lines between commercial interests and state surveillance are often blurred, as governments and corporations collaborate in sharing and utilizing data. This blurring of lines is inherently problematic and necessitates greater transparency and regulatory oversight.

The ethical implications of these technologies are profound. The constant monitoring of individuals' behavior, without their informed consent, raises serious questions about autonomy, freedom, and dignity. The potential for bias and discrimination in algorithms further compounds the ethical concerns. Algorithms trained on biased data will perpetuate and amplify existing inequalities, leading to unfair and discriminatory outcomes. The lack of accountability and transparency in the development and deployment of surveillance technologies makes it difficult to address these ethical concerns effectively.

Addressing the challenges posed by surveillance technologies requires a multi-pronged approach. Firstly, it requires strengthening legal frameworks to regulate the collection, use, and sharing of personal data. Legislation needs to be comprehensive, addressing the specific risks posed by different surveillance technologies, while carefully balancing the need for public safety with the protection of privacy rights. This includes establishing clear guidelines for data collection, storage, and use, alongside mechanisms for redress in cases of data misuse. Secondly, there needs to be greater transparency and accountability in the development and deployment of these technologies. This includes making algorithms used in predictive policing and social scoring systems more transparent, allowing for independent audits and assessments to identify and mitigate biases. Thirdly, there is a need for increased public awareness and education. Citizens need to be educated about the risks posed by surveillance technologies and empowered to protect their privacy. This includes providing resources and tools to individuals to understand and manage their digital footprint.

Ultimately, the fight against the erosion of privacy in the age of surveillance technologies is a fight for the very soul of democracy. It is a battle that requires vigilance, a robust legal framework, technological literacy, and a collective commitment to safeguarding our fundamental rights and freedoms. The potential consequences of inaction are simply too dire to ignore. The unchecked proliferation of these technologies poses an existential threat to democratic values, making it crucial to engage in a sustained and concerted effort to protect our freedoms before it is too late. The future of privacy, and indeed the future of democracy, hangs in the balance.

INTERNET AS A TOOL FOR CONTROL AND CENSORSHIP

The internet, initially envisioned as a decentralized, democratizing force, has ironically become a potent instrument for control and censorship in the hands of authoritarian regimes and powerful corporations. The very architecture that promised open access and free exchange of information has been repurposed to restrict dissent and manipulate public opinion. This transformation is not accidental; it's a calculated strategy, meticulously executed through a combination of sophisticated technologies and legal maneuvering.

One of the most insidious aspects of this control is the manipulation of search engine algorithms. Search results, which often serve as the primary gateway to information for billions of users, can be subtly — and sometimes not so subtly — manipulated to favor certain narratives and suppress others. Governments and corporations alike wield this power, using sophisticated techniques to influence the information landscape. They can strategically boost articles aligned with their interests while burying dissenting viewpoints, creating a biased information ecosystem that shapes public perception and limits access to alternative perspectives. This manipulation is often invisible to the average user, who unknowingly receives a curated and potentially skewed version of reality.

The deployment of sophisticated filtering and blocking technologies further intensifies the internet's role as a tool for censorship. Governments employ "Great Firewall"-style systems to block access to websites, social media platforms, and online resources deemed subversive or critical of the regime. This digital iron curtain prevents citizens from accessing information from outside sources, fostering a climate of isolation and reinforcing the official narrative. The sophistication of these firewalls is constantly evolving, making it increasingly difficult to circumvent their restrictions. Circumvention methods, such as VPNs and proxy servers, are constantly being developed, yet the cat-and-mouse game between those seeking freedom of information and those attempting to suppress it is a perpetual struggle.

Beyond the outright blocking of websites, governments increasingly utilize more subtle forms of censorship, including the manipulation of social media algorithms, the deletion of critical posts, and the harassment of online activists. These tactics, often deployed indirectly by government-linked entities or through the complicity of social media companies, create a climate of self-censorship. Individuals fear retribution for expressing dissenting opinions online, leading to a chilling effect on free speech and the stifling of critical debate. The impact extends beyond the realm of overt political dissent, influencing even seemingly innocuous conversations and interactions.

The issue is exacerbated by the lack of transparency in the algorithms that govern social media platforms. These opaque algorithms, often developed in secrecy by private companies, dictate what information users see, the order in which they see it, and which voices are amplified and which are silenced. This lack of transparency makes it nearly impossible to determine whether algorithmic bias is contributing to the suppression of dissent or to the amplification of misinformation. The consequence is a distorted information environment where truth is increasingly indistinguishable from propaganda.

The increasing use of automated content moderation systems raises concerns about the potential for bias and the suppression of legitimate expression. While these systems are designed to identify and remove harmful content, including hate speech and misinformation, their application is often flawed and prone to error. They can inadvertently censor legitimate criticism, thereby undermining free speech and silencing dissenting voices. The lack of human oversight and the inherent limitations of AI-based moderation systems further compound this problem.

The surveillance capabilities of the internet further contribute to its role in authoritarian control. Governments and corporations utilize mass data collection techniques to monitor online activities, tracking individuals' browsing history, social media interactions, and online communications. This data is then used to identify and target potential dissidents, allowing for preemptive suppression of dissent before it can gain traction. The ability to track and analyze vast amounts of data allows authorities to identify patterns of behavior and to predict future actions, enabling them to anticipate and neutralize potential threats.

The pervasiveness of surveillance is amplified by the integration of the internet into almost every aspect of our daily lives. From smart devices in our homes to the ubiquitous smartphones we carry, we are constantly generating data that can be collected and analyzed. The potential for misuse of this data is immense, particularly in the hands of authoritarian regimes. This creates a chilling effect, leading individuals to self-censor their online activities and limit their expression for fear of surveillance and retribution.

The commercial interests of corporations further complicate the issue. Large technology companies, often seeking to maximize profits and maintain access to lucrative markets, are increasingly willing to cooperate with governments in censoring online content and providing access to user data. This cooperation, often shrouded in secrecy, enables the suppression of dissent and the erosion of privacy rights on a massive scale. The intertwining of commercial interests and political power makes it increasingly difficult to differentiate between legitimate commercial activity and complicity in authoritarian control.

The implications of this situation are profound and far-reaching. The erosion of freedom of expression and access to information online has a direct impact on the ability of citizens to engage in democratic processes, to hold their governments accountable, and to challenge power. It undermines the very foundations of democratic societies, creating a climate of fear and self-censorship that stifles innovation and inhibits progress. The internet, once a symbol of liberation and freedom, is becoming a tool for control, hindering the advancement of human rights and undermining the principles of free societies.

Combating this insidious trend requires a multifaceted approach. This involves strengthening legal frameworks to protect freedom of expression and privacy online, advocating for greater transparency in algorithmic processes, promoting digital literacy and media literacy to enable citizens to critically assess information, supporting organizations that work to bypass censorship, and holding corporations accountable for their role in enabling authoritarian control. This is not simply a technological challenge; it is a fight for the future of democracy itself, a fight that demands a collective and sustained effort from individuals, civil society, and governments alike. The future of a free and open internet, and the future of freedom itself, hangs in the balance. The stakes couldn't be higher.

"AI" AND THE AUTOMATION OF OPPRESSION

The terrifying implications of the internet's role in authoritarian control extend far beyond the manipulation of search algorithms and the deployment of firewalls. We are now entering a new and profoundly disturbing era where artificial intelligence (AI) is rapidly becoming a tool for the automation of oppression, amplifying the existing threats to democracy and individual liberties on an unprecedented scale. The potential for AI to be weaponized against its own creators is a terrifying prospect that demands immediate and critical attention.

The rise of predictive policing, fueled by AI algorithms, provides a stark illustration of this emerging threat. These systems analyze vast datasets of historical crime statistics, demographic information, and even social media activity to predict the likelihood of future criminal activity in specific locations or among particular individuals. While proponents argue that such systems enhance law enforcement efficiency and reduce crime rates, critics highlight the inherent biases embedded within the data used to train these algorithms. These biases, often reflecting existing societal inequalities, can lead to disproportionate policing in marginalized communities, perpetuating cycles of oppression and undermining the principle of equal justice under the law. The very notion of preemptively targeting individuals based on probabilistic predictions of future behavior raises profound ethical questions about due process and the presumption of innocence. The algorithm, in essence, becomes a judge and jury, operating without the fundamental safeguards of a fair legal system. Furthermore, the opacity of these algorithms makes it difficult, if not impossible, to understand how they arrive at their conclusions, fostering a lack of transparency and accountability. This opacity allows for potential misuse and discrimination to go unchecked.

The development and deployment of social credit systems represent another alarming example of AI-driven oppression. These systems, already operational in several countries, utilize AI to track and evaluate citizens' behavior across a range of areas, including financial transactions, social media activity, and even adherence to government regulations. The data is then used to assign an individual a "social credit score," which determines access to services, opportunities, and even basic freedoms. Individuals with low scores may face restrictions on travel, employment, education, and even access to essential healthcare. The chilling effect of such systems is immense, incentivizing conformity and silencing dissent. Critics argue that such systems are inherently undemocratic, undermining fundamental human rights and fostering a climate of fear and self-censorship. The potential for misuse is also significant, with the risk of political opponents being unfairly targeted or marginalized through manipulation of their scores. The lack of transparency and accountability in these systems further exacerbates the concerns. The power to determine an individual's fate rests in the hands of an algorithm, making individuals vulnerable to the biases embedded within the system and susceptible to arbitrary manipulation.

Targeted surveillance, enabled by AI-powered facial recognition technology and sophisticated data analytics, presents yet another grave threat to individual liberties. These systems can track individuals' movements, identify them in crowds, and even analyze their facial expressions to infer their emotional state. Governments and corporations can use this information to monitor citizens' activities, identify dissidents, and suppress protests. The pervasiveness of this technology, coupled with the lack of effective legal safeguards, creates a climate of fear and self-censorship that restricts individual freedom of movement and expression. This chilling effect extends beyond political activism, impacting everyday life and the ability to express oneself freely without fear of constant surveillance and potential reprisal. The potential for misuse extends to the targeting of specific groups based on their religion, ethnicity, or political beliefs.

The ethical implications of using AI for social control are profound and far-reaching. The unchecked deployment of AI-powered surveillance and control systems raises fundamental questions about privacy, autonomy, and human dignity. The development and implementation of these technologies must be guided by a strong ethical framework that prioritizes human rights and democratic values. However, the current regulatory landscape is inadequate to address the rapidly evolving nature of AI technology and its potential for misuse. The lack of international cooperation and consistent standards creates a dangerous environment where technology is developing faster than the capacity to regulate it, creating an imbalance that threatens the very foundations of free societies.

The need for robust regulation to prevent the misuse of AI for oppressive purposes is paramount. This regulation must address several key issues, including the transparency of algorithms, the accountability of developers and deployers of AI systems, and the protection of individual rights and freedoms. Moreover, international collaboration is essential to establish common standards and mechanisms for oversight to prevent a global race to the bottom, where countries compete to implement increasingly invasive AI-driven surveillance systems without regard for ethical considerations or human rights.

The challenge lies not only in developing effective regulations but also in ensuring their enforcement and the accountability of those who violate them. The opacity of many AI systems makes it difficult to determine whether they are being used ethically or whether their biases are perpetuating existing inequalities. This lack of transparency needs to be addressed through mandatory audits, independent oversight mechanisms, and increased public access to information about how these systems operate. The failure to address these challenges will result in an alarming erosion of fundamental rights and a future where technology is used to silence dissent, control populations, and consolidate power in the hands of the few, exacerbating the already precarious state of democratic values in a world increasingly dominated by technological advancements. The fight for a future where technology serves humanity, rather than oppresses it, requires urgent and concerted action from governments, civil society, and individuals alike. The stakes are nothing less than the future of freedom itself.

CRYPTOCURRENCIES AND DECENTRALIZED RESISTANCE

Cryptocurrencies, built on blockchain's transparent ledger, offer a financial system beyond government control, potentially shielding dissenters' funds. This decentralized finance empowers individuals to transact freely. However, the anonymity afforded by cryptocurrencies can be exploited by criminal elements, undermining their positive potential for resistance. Regulation remains a crucial consideration. The ongoing struggle between centralized power and decentralized technologies creates a complex landscape, ripe with both risk and opportunity for shaping a more equitable future. Further exploration is needed.

At its core, the promise of cryptocurrencies lies in their decentralization. Unlike traditional fiat currencies, controlled by central banks and governments, cryptocurrencies operate on a distributed ledger technology—the blockchain—making them resistant to censorship and manipulation by a single entity. This fundamental characteristic directly challenges the power dynamics inherent in authoritarian regimes which often exert control through the manipulation of financial systems. By providing an alternative financial infrastructure, cryptocurrencies enable individuals to transact outside the purview of government oversight, fostering financial independence and resilience against economic sanctions or restrictions imposed by oppressive regimes.

The implications of this financial independence are profound. Consider, for instance, a country where the government restricts access to foreign currency or severely limits the ability of citizens to transfer funds internationally. In such a scenario, cryptocurrencies can serve as a lifeline, allowing citizens to bypass these restrictions and access global markets, participate in the global economy, and support independent media or organizations critical of the regime. This capability is not merely theoretical. We have already witnessed instances where cryptocurrencies have been utilized in this manner, providing a critical channel for financial support to dissidents and activists facing suppression and persecution. The ability to donate or receive funds anonymously, or with a level of pseudonymous identity protection, provides a layer of security essential for those operating in high-risk environments.

Additionally, the use of blockchain technology extends beyond simple financial transactions. The immutable and transparent nature of the blockchain provides a secure platform for storing and sharing information, thereby challenging state-controlled narratives and promoting freedom of expression. Decentralized platforms, built upon blockchain technology, offer a space for individuals to communicate and share information without fear of censorship or surveillance by authoritarian regimes. This is particularly crucial in countries where traditional media outlets are heavily censored or controlled by the state. Decentralized platforms can provide a vital alternative, allowing citizens to access a wider range of information and perspectives, fostering a more informed and empowered citizenry—a crucial counterweight to the state's monopoly on information.

However, the relationship between cryptocurrencies and decentralized resistance is not without its complexities and limitations. The inherent anonymity associated with some cryptocurrencies can also be exploited for illicit activities, raising concerns about money laundering and the financing of terrorism. This duality presents a significant challenge, as governments and regulatory bodies often seek to regulate cryptocurrencies with the aim of curbing criminal activity, inadvertently undermining their potential for promoting freedom and dissent. Finding a balance between ensuring security and protecting the ability of cryptocurrencies to facilitate resistance is a crucial task that demands careful consideration. The conversation requires a nuanced approach that differentiates between legitimate use of cryptocurrencies for fostering freedom of expression and their potential for misuse by criminal actors.

Another significant limitation is the technological literacy required to effectively utilize cryptocurrencies and decentralized platforms. In many parts of the world, particularly in regions ruled by authoritarian regimes, access to technology and digital literacy are limited. This digital divide creates an inequality that limits the reach and effectiveness of these technologies as tools for resistance. Bridging this digital divide requires concerted efforts to educate and empower individuals, particularly marginalized communities, to utilize these technologies effectively.

Moreover, the volatility of cryptocurrency markets presents a significant challenge. The fluctuating value of cryptocurrencies can impact their usability as a stable medium of exchange, making them less reliable as a tool for long-term financial planning or support for sustained resistance movements. This inherent instability can limit their effectiveness as a tool for economic empowerment and mobilization. Furthermore, authoritarian regimes are actively exploring ways to regulate and control cryptocurrencies, potentially undermining their utility as a tool for circumventing state control. The technological arms race between those seeking to utilize cryptocurrencies for resistance and those seeking to suppress them is ongoing, and the outcome is far from certain.

Despite these limitations, the potential of cryptocurrencies and blockchain technology to empower individuals and facilitate resistance against authoritarian regimes remains undeniable. As technology continues to evolve, so too will the methods employed by both those who seek to suppress freedom and those who strive to defend it. The ongoing development of decentralized technologies and the creative exploration of their applications by activists and civil society organizations continue to hold the potential to reshape the landscape of political power. The battle for the future of freedom is being fought on multiple fronts, and the technological front is proving to be a particularly vital one.

It is important to acknowledge that the decentralized resistance enabled by cryptocurrencies is not a panacea. It is a tool, albeit a powerful one, that must be used strategically and in conjunction with other forms of resistance. The fight for freedom requires a multifaceted approach, incorporating both technological innovation and traditional forms of activism and political engagement. The role of cryptocurrencies and blockchain technology is to augment, not replace, these other vital components. Ultimately, the effectiveness of these tools depends not only on their technical capabilities but also on the strategic acumen and organizational capacity of those who utilize them. The successful deployment of cryptocurrencies and decentralized platforms in the fight against authoritarianism will require a concerted effort from activists, developers, and policymakers alike, working collaboratively to overcome the inherent challenges and maximize the potential for positive change. The challenge lies in leveraging the technology's potential while mitigating its risks, ensuring that it truly serves as a tool for empowerment and freedom, not another weapon in the hands of the powerful. The ongoing evolution of this technological landscape demands continuous vigilance, critical analysis, and unwavering commitment to the principles of human rights and democratic values. The future of decentralized resistance, and indeed, the future of freedom itself, depends upon it.

THE DIGITAL DIVIDE AND ITS IMPACT ON DEMOCRACY

The preceding discussion highlighted the potential of decentralized technologies to challenge authoritarian control. However, the promise of these tools remains largely unrealized for a significant portion of the global population. The stark reality is that the digital divide, the chasm separating those with access to technology and the internet from those without, profoundly undermines the potential of these technologies to foster democratic participation and access to information. This divide isn't simply a matter of convenience; it's a fundamental barrier to meaningful engagement in the digital age, exacerbating existing inequalities and strengthening the hand of authoritarian regimes.

The digital divide manifests itself in numerous ways. In some regions, the lack of physical infrastructure—the absence of internet connectivity, reliable electricity, and even functioning devices—presents a formidable obstacle. Imagine a rural community in sub-Saharan Africa, where access to the internet is limited to a single, unreliable connection in the town center, or where electricity is intermittent. In such contexts, the very notion of participating in online discussions, accessing crucial information, or organizing digital resistance becomes a monumental challenge. The economic constraints faced by these communities, often characterized by widespread poverty and limited access to education, further compound the issue, creating a feedback loop that traps them in a cycle of technological exclusion.

Beyond physical infrastructure, the digital divide extends to digital literacy. Even when access to technology exists, the ability to effectively utilize it requires a certain level of digital literacy. This encompasses a range of skills, from basic computer operation and internet navigation to understanding online security and critical evaluation of online information. A significant portion of the global population lacks these skills, rendering them vulnerable to manipulation and misinformation. Authoritarian regimes cleverly exploit this vulnerability, deploying sophisticated propaganda campaigns through social media and other online platforms, while simultaneously suppressing dissenting voices.

The consequences of this digital illiteracy are profound. Individuals lacking digital literacy are more susceptible to propaganda and disinformation, hindering their ability to make informed decisions about their political leaders and policies. This, in turn, undermines the very foundation of democratic participation. The inability to access and critically analyze information effectively contributes to a climate of political apathy and disengagement. Furthermore, it limits the ability of citizens to hold their leaders accountable, and strengthens the grip of power held by those who control the flow of information.

The impact of the digital divide extends beyond individual citizens; it directly affects the ability of civil society organizations and independent media outlets to operate effectively. These organizations often rely on digital platforms to communicate with their audiences, mobilize support, and coordinate their activities. When a significant portion of the population lacks access to these platforms, the reach and impact of these organizations are severely limited. Consequently, the ability of civil society to act as a counterweight to authoritarian power is weakened, leaving a void that authoritarian regimes readily fill.

Consider the case of China, where the government exercises strict control over the internet through its "Great Firewall." While technological infrastructure is relatively advanced, the government's control over information flow, combined with a system of surveillance and censorship, significantly restricts access to independent news sources and critical political discourse. This restricts not only the flow of information to the general population but also the ability of domestic and international human rights organizations to document and report on human rights abuses within the country.

Similarly, in many authoritarian regimes in the Middle East and North Africa, internet access is frequently restricted during periods of political unrest or social protest. These restrictions aim to prevent the dissemination of information and the organization of protests, effectively silencing dissent and preventing collective action. This underscores how the control of technology and information plays a crucial role in maintaining authoritarian rule. The digital divide not only limits access to information but also limits the ability to organize collective action.

Bridging this digital divide requires a multifaceted approach. It calls for significant investments in infrastructure development, including expanding internet access in underserved communities, particularly in rural areas. This requires not only the physical infrastructure—laying fiber optic cables, building cell towers—but also addressing underlying issues of electricity supply and affordability. Simply providing access is insufficient; we must also address the question of affordability. Internet access should not be a luxury afforded only to the wealthy but a fundamental right, accessible to all regardless of their socioeconomic status.

Equally critical is the development of digital literacy programs. These programs must be tailored to the specific needs and circumstances of different communities, considering factors such as age, education level, and language barriers. The focus should be not merely on acquiring technical skills but also on cultivating critical thinking and media literacy. This ensures that individuals can effectively navigate the complexities of the digital world, avoiding misinformation and participating effectively in online political discussions.

It's crucial to foster a culture of digital inclusion. This necessitates involving communities in the design and implementation of technology initiatives, recognizing the specific needs and challenges faced by different groups. Top-down approaches often fail to adequately address the underlying issues, exacerbating the digital divide. By engaging communities as active participants, we can develop sustainable solutions that address the specific needs of those who are most affected.

International cooperation also plays a crucial role. Governments, international organizations, and non-governmental organizations must work together to support infrastructure development and digital literacy programs in countries where the digital divide is most severe. This requires collaborative efforts, sharing best practices, and providing financial and technical assistance to developing countries. Furthermore, international pressure can be exerted on authoritarian regimes to improve internet access and freedom of information, promoting a more inclusive and democratic digital landscape.

The digital divide isn't simply a technological problem; it's a social and political one. Overcoming this divide requires a concerted effort from all stakeholders to address the underlying economic and social inequalities that exacerbate it. By investing in infrastructure, fostering digital literacy, and promoting digital inclusion, we can create a more equitable and democratic digital landscape, empowering citizens to participate fully in the globalized world and challenging the pervasive influence of authoritarian regimes. Ignoring the digital divide is not just a neglect of technological advancement; it is a betrayal of democratic principles and a tacit endorsement of authoritarian control. The future of democracy hinges on bridging this chasm, ensuring that the transformative potential of technology is available to all.

THE LUNATIC'S GUIDE TO SANITY

DISSENT IN THE FACE OF AUTHORITARIANISM

In times of political crisis, when the familiar comforts of democracy erode and the icy grip of authoritarianism tightens its hold, the voices of dissent are often labeled as the ravings of lunatics. To speak out against the rising tide of control, to question the narratives spun by those in power, is to invite ridicule, ostracization, and even persecution. Yet, it is precisely in these moments that the "lunatic's guide to sanity" becomes essential, a compass pointing towards the preservation of freedom and the enduring value of truth.

Authoritarianism is often associated with the promise of order during times of chaos or perceived disorder, the appeal of strong leadership during uncertain periods, and the concept of sovereignty in contemporary contexts. When the existing political system falters, burdened by corruption, inequality, or external threats, the siren song of a decisive, unified force can be powerfully seductive. People yearn for stability, for a clear path forward, even if it means sacrificing certain liberties. However, the history of the 20th century, littered with the wreckage of totalitarian regimes, serves as a stark reminder of the devastating outcomes that can arise from surrendering individual freedoms to the perceived wisdom of a single leader or party. Censorship, propaganda, the suppression of dissent, and the erosion of legal safeguards are all hallmarks of authoritarianism, ultimately leading to the systematic violation of human rights and the crushing of individual potential.

Why, then, is it important to be the outcast, to speak out against the devastating outcomes that can come from a dictatorship, even when branded a "lunatic"? Because silence, in the face of injustice, is complicity. When the foundations of a free society are threatened, the responsibility to defend them falls upon each and every citizen. Speaking truth to power, even when it is unwelcome, is not an act of madness, but an act of courage and civic responsibility. It is a refusal to be silenced by fear, an affirmation of the enduring power of individual conscience.

The "lunatics," the dissenters, the outcasts, are the canaries in the coal mine of democracy. They are the first to feel the poisonous fumes of authoritarianism, and their cries serve as a warning to others. They see the subtle shifts in language, the erosion of norms, and the gradual normalization of injustice that others may miss. They understand that unchecked power corrupts, and that the only safeguard against tyranny is a vigilant and engaged citizenry.

Moreover, dissent challenges the narrative of inevitability often employed by authoritarian regimes. By questioning the status quo, by offering alternative perspectives, the "lunatics" disrupt the carefully constructed image of absolute control. They demonstrate that resistance is possible, that the dominant ideology is not monolithic, and that there is hope for a future where freedom and justice prevail. They remind us that the emperor has no clothes, even if everyone else is afraid to admit it.

Fighting against such systems, even when considered "lunatics," is not just a matter of principle, it is a matter of survival. Authoritarianism, by its very nature, seeks to eliminate any opposition, to silence dissenting voices, and to control every aspect of human life. To passively accept such a system is to condemn oneself and future generations to a life of subjugation, fear, and intellectual stagnation.

The fight against authoritarianism requires resilience, perseverance, and a willingness to endure ridicule and hardship. It demands the formation of alliances, the mobilization of public opinion, and the use of every available tool to resist oppression. It requires a commitment to truth, even when it is unpopular, and an unwavering belief in the power of individual agency.

The "lunatic's guide to sanity" is a call to action, a reminder that in times of political crisis, the most rational response is often to question the prevailing narrative and to speak out against injustice. To be the outcast, to be labeled a "lunatic," may be a difficult path, but it is a necessary one for the preservation of freedom and the defense of democracy. For it is the "lunatics," the dissenters, who ultimately hold the key to sanity in a world threatened by the seductive and ultimately destructive forces of authoritarianism. Their voices, though often marginalized, are the beacons of hope that guide us towards a future where justice, equality, and individual liberty prevail.

But beyond simply identifying the warning signs and understanding the importance of dissent, the "lunatic's guide" must become our guide for strategies that will help us navigate the treacherous landscape of authoritarianism. It is a handbook for maintaining sanity in an insane world, a guide for fostering resistance even when hope seems lost.

One crucial element of this guide is the cultivation of independent thought. Authoritarian regimes thrive on conformity, on the unquestioning acceptance of state-sanctioned narratives. To resist this, one must actively seek out diverse sources of information, engage in critical analysis, and develop the ability to discern truth from falsehood. This requires intellectual rigor, a willingness to challenge one's own biases, and a commitment to lifelong learning. It means reading history, philosophy, and literature that offer alternative perspectives and challenge the prevailing ideology. It means engaging in meaningful conversations with people who hold different viewpoints, even when those conversations are uncomfortable.

Another vital tool in the "lunatic's" arsenal is the power of community. Authoritarianism seeks to isolate individuals, to break down social bonds, and to create a climate of fear and suspicion. Building strong, resilient communities is therefore an act of resistance. These communities can provide mutual support, share resources, and coordinate collective action. They can also serve as safe spaces for dissent, where individuals can express their concerns and ideas without fear of reprisal. The formation of these communities, whether they are based on shared interests, geographical proximity, or political affiliation, is a vital way to counter the isolating effects of authoritarian rule. Furthermore, these communities become the breeding ground for future leaders and activists who will carry the torch of freedom forward.

Authoritarian regimes often target art and culture, recognizing their power to challenge authority and inspire dissent. By supporting artists, writers, musicians, and filmmakers who offer alternative perspectives, we can keep the flame of creativity alive and resist the stifling effects of censorship. Art can be a powerful tool for exposing injustice, promoting empathy, and fostering a sense of shared humanity. It can also serve as a form of catharsis, allowing individuals to process their emotions and find hope in the face of adversity. Underground art movements, samizdat literature, and defiant musical performances all become potent symbols of resistance and a testament to the enduring human spirit.

We must advocate for strategic non-violent resistance. While authoritarian regimes often rely on violence and intimidation to maintain control, non-violent tactics can be remarkably effective in challenging their legitimacy and undermining their authority. These tactics can include peaceful protests, boycotts, strikes, civil disobedience, and the use of humor and satire to expose the absurdity of the regime. Non-violent resistance requires discipline, courage, and a deep understanding of the regime's vulnerabilities. It also requires a commitment to non-violence, even in the face of provocation. The success of non-violent movements throughout history, from the Civil Rights Movement in the United States to the Solidarity movement in Poland, demonstrates the power of ordinary people to challenge even the most oppressive regimes.

Through the "lunatic's guide" it's our duty to recognize the importance of maintaining hope and resilience. The fight against authoritarianism can be a long and arduous one, and there will be times when it feels like the forces of oppression are insurmountable. It is during these times that it is essential to draw strength from one's values, to connect with others who share one's beliefs, and to remember that even small acts of resistance can make a difference. Hope is not simply a naive optimism; it is a conscious choice to believe in the possibility of a better future, even when the present seems bleak. Resilience is the ability to bounce back from setbacks, to learn from one's mistakes, and to continue fighting for what is right, even when the odds are stacked against you.

The "lunatic's guide" is, therefore, not just a guide to resisting authoritarianism, but also a guide to living a meaningful and fulfilling life in the face of oppression. It is a request to the enduring human capacity for courage, compassion, and hope, and a reminder that united even the darkest nights eventually give way to the dawn.

ESSENTIAL GUIDE

Navigating the Treacherous Landscape of Authoritarianism

PRACTICAL STRATEGIES FOR SURVIVAL AND RESISTANCE

Authoritarianism, with its iron grip on power and suppression of dissent, presents a formidable challenge to those who value freedom, justice, and individual autonomy. It is a landscape fraught with peril, where even the slightest misstep can have dire consequences. Navigating this treacherous terrain requires not only a deep understanding of the regime's mechanisms of control but also a carefully considered strategy that balances survival with the pursuit of meaningful resistance. This chapter will explore practical strategies, both philosophical and political, for navigating the complexities of authoritarianism, acknowledging the inherent risks and focusing on approaches that aim to preserve individual integrity while subtly undermining the regime's authority.

- **CULTIVATING INNER RESILIENCE...** One of the most crucial aspects of surviving under authoritarianism is cultivating inner resilience and maintaining personal integrity. This involves safeguarding one's moral compass, practicing self-care, and finding pockets of freedom within the confines of a restricted environment. Philosophically, this can be informed by Stoicism, which emphasizes focusing on what is within our control – our thoughts, actions, and values – and accepting what is not, such as the actions of the regime. By prioritizing inner peace and adhering to a personal code of ethics, individuals can resist the corrosive effects of state-sponsored propaganda and maintain a sense of self-worth even in the face of oppression. Practical strategies include cultivating close relationships with trusted individuals, engaging in activities that promote mental and emotional well-being, and discreetly preserving cultural and historical knowledge that the regime seeks to erase.

- **DEVELOPING SOCIAL NETWORKS...** Building upon this foundation of inner strength, a critical strategy is the formation and nurturing of social networks. Authoritarian regimes thrive on isolating individuals and suppressing collective action. Counteracting this requires fostering clandestine networks of trust and solidarity. These networks can be built around shared values, professional affiliations, or even seemingly innocuous social activities. The strength of these networks lies in their ability to share information, provide mutual support, and coordinate small acts of resistance. Philosophically, this aligns with communitarian values, emphasizing the importance of social bonds and collective action in promoting human flourishing. Practically, this can involve organizing small study groups, participating in community projects, or simply offering a listening ear to those who are suffering.

- **ADOPTING TACTICS OF STRATEGIC AMBIGUITY AND DISSIMULATION...** Another key strategy lies in openly confronting the regime, which can be suicidal, but passively complying with its demands also reinforces its power. A more effective approach involves employing subtle forms of resistance that are difficult for the authorities to detect. This might involve feigning loyalty while subtly undermining the regime's propaganda, engaging in acts of non-compliance under the guise of incompetence, or using humor and satire to expose the regime's absurdities. Philosophically, this resonates with the ideas of Machiavelli, who advocated for the use of deception and pragmatism in the pursuit of political goals. Practically, this can involve using coded language in online communication, subtly challenging the regime's narratives in everyday conversations, or engaging in acts of civil disobedience that are difficult to prosecute.

- **IT'S ESSENTIAL TO PRESERVE AND PROPAGATE INDEPENDENT INFORMATION...** Authoritarian regimes rely on controlling the flow of information to maintain their grip on power. Breaking this control requires finding alternative sources of information and disseminating them discreetly. This might involve accessing foreign news websites using VPNs, sharing banned books and articles through encrypted channels, or documenting human rights abuses and sharing them with international organizations. Philosophically, this aligns with the principles of free speech and access to information, which are essential for a functioning democracy. Practically, this can involve setting up anonymous social media accounts, creating underground libraries, or using secure communication channels to share news and information.

- **IT'S CRUCIAL TO FOCUS ON LONG-TERM GOALS AND AVOID IMPULSIVE ACTIONS...** Authoritarianism is rarely overthrown overnight. Meaningful change requires a sustained and strategic effort. This means avoiding actions that could unnecessarily endanger oneself or others and focusing on strategies that can gradually erode the regime's power. This includes educating future generations about the importance of freedom and democracy, supporting civil society organizations that promote human rights, and building international alliances to pressure the regime to reform. Philosophically, this requires a sense of historical perspective and an understanding that the struggle for freedom is a long and arduous one. Practically, it means focusing on building sustainable structures of resistance that can withstand the regime's efforts to suppress them.

- **PROTECTING AND PRESERVING DEMOCRATIC INSTITUTIONS, EVEN UNDER DURESS...** This includes defending the rule of law, advocating for fair elections, and upholding the independence of the judiciary. Supporting lawyers and human rights activists who are challenging unjust laws and defending political prisoners is essential. Participating in electoral processes, even if they are compromised, can provide opportunities to expose fraud and challenge the legitimacy of the regime. Furthermore, documenting and disseminating information about human rights abuses and corruption can help hold the regime accountable and galvanize international pressure.

- **PRESERVING CULTURAL MEMORY AND ARTISTIC EXPRESSION…** Authoritarian regimes often attempt to rewrite history and suppress dissenting artistic voices. Maintaining and celebrating cultural traditions, supporting independent artists, and preserving historical documents can serve as powerful acts of resistance. Storytelling, music, and art can provide a platform for expressing dissent, fostering solidarity, and reminding people of the values the regime is trying to suppress. These acts of cultural resistance can keep the spirit of freedom alive, even in the darkest of times.

- **STRATEGIC NON-VIOLENT RESISTANCE…** offers a powerful tool for challenging authoritarian regimes. Gene Sharp's work on nonviolent action provides a framework for understanding how ordinary people can undermine the power of even the most repressive governments. This involves strategies such as boycotts, strikes, civil disobedience, and the creation of parallel institutions. Strategic non-violent resistance requires careful planning, disciplined execution, and a deep understanding of the regime's vulnerabilities. It also requires a commitment to non-violence, even in the face of provocation, as violence can often be used as a pretext for further repression.

Navigating the landscape of authoritarianism is a long and arduous journey. There is no single, foolproof strategy for achieving freedom. However, by cultivating independent thought, strengthening civil society, protecting democratic institutions, preserving cultural memory, and employing strategic non-violent resistance, individuals and communities can undermine the power of authoritarian regimes and create opportunities for a more just and equitable future. The success of these strategies depends not only on the courage and resilience of those who resist, but also on the support and solidarity of the international community. The fight against authoritarianism is a global struggle, and the freedom of one depends on the freedom of all.

In conclusion, overcoming the unpredictable landscape of authoritarianism demands a careful balance of philosophical conviction and practical strategies. By cultivating inner resilience, nurturing social networks, adopting tactics of strategic ambiguity, preserving and disseminating independent information, and focusing on long-term goals, individuals can survive and resist the oppressive forces that threaten their freedom. While the risks are undeniable, the potential rewards of a more just and equitable society make the struggle worthwhile. The key lies in understanding the regime's weaknesses, exploiting its vulnerabilities, and building a resilient network of resistance that can ultimately pave the way for a more democratic future. While overt revolution may not always be possible or desirable, the slow, persistent erosion of authoritarian power through subtle acts of resistance can ultimately prove more effective in the long run. The journey is fraught with challenges, but the pursuit of freedom and justice remains a timeless and essential human endeavor.

Embracing The *Outsider*

THE POWER OF NONCONFORMITY

"The Lunatic's Guide to Sanity," as imagined in this context, presents a radical yet vital argument: embracing the outsider, the nonconformist, is not a sign of madness but a pathway to genuine sanity, especially in times of crisis. This chapter challenges the deeply ingrained societal pressure to conform, to fit neatly within pre-defined boxes, and instead champions the courage to question, to challenge, and ultimately, to dissent. It argues that the very act of refusing to blindly accept the status quo, of embracing intellectual isolation if necessary, is not only a necessary act of self-preservation but also a morally imperative contribution to societal progress.

The prevailing notion that "fitting in" is a virtue is insidious. It fosters intellectual stagnation, stifles creativity, and ultimately, can blind us to injustice. Societal norms, often presented as objective truths, are frequently constructs, shaped by power structures and perpetuated by fear of disrupting the established order. In times of crisis, be it economic turmoil, political instability, or moral decay, these norms are often exposed as fragile facades, incapable of providing genuine solutions. This is precisely when the outsider, the "lunatic" who dares to question the crumbling edifice, becomes crucial. They offer alternative perspectives, challenge flawed assumptions, and pave the way for innovative solutions that would otherwise be dismissed or ignored. Their value isn't simply in their dissent, however, but in the critical lens they apply to the world, a lens unclouded by the pressure to conform.

History is replete with examples of individuals who were ostracized, labeled as mad, or persecuted for their unconventional views. Galileo Galilei, condemned for his heretical belief in a heliocentric universe, stands as a potent symbol of the conflict between established dogma and scientific truth. Socrates, the gadfly of Athens, was sentenced to death for challenging the prevailing wisdom and corrupting the youth. Joan of Arc, a peasant girl claiming divine guidance, was burned at the stake for defying societal gender roles and political authority. These figures, initially condemned as deviants, are now revered as visionaries who dared to challenge the limitations of their time. However, it is not enough to simply acknowledge their historical significance; we must also understand the mechanisms that led to their persecution. The fear of the unknown, the resistance to change, and the desire to maintain existing power structures all contribute to the marginalization of those who challenge the status quo.

Their power lay not in their ability to conform but in their unwavering commitment to truth as they understood it. They possessed the intellectual courage to confront the societal pressure, the fear of social isolation, and even the threat of physical harm, to articulate their beliefs. They understood that genuine progress requires challenging conventional wisdom, questioning the assumptions that underpin the status quo, and imagining alternative possibilities. Their ostracism was not a sign of their failure but a testament to their courage, a badge of honor signifying their refusal to be silenced. This courage is not innate; it is cultivated through critical thinking, self-awareness, and a deep understanding of the principles of justice and fairness. It requires a willingness to stand alone, to face ridicule, and to endure hardship in the pursuit of truth.

Nonconformity is not simply about intellectual rebellion; it is also a crucial act of moral responsibility. When injustice prevails, when the powerful abuse their authority, or when society drifts toward moral bankruptcy, the act of conformity becomes complicity. The bystander effect thrives on the silence of those who fear standing out, who worry about the social cost of speaking truth to power. True sanity, the "Lunatic's Guide" suggests, lies in rejecting this complicity. It lies in recognizing that silence is not neutrality but an active endorsement of the prevailing injustice. The nonconformist, in this context, becomes a moral compass, guiding society back towards principles of ethical conduct and social responsibility. They remind us that we are all accountable for the actions of our society, and that we cannot simply stand idly by while injustice occurs.

However, embracing the outsider does not necessarily mean adopting a contrarian stance for its own sake. It requires critical thinking, rigorous self-reflection, and a genuine commitment to seeking truth, even when it is uncomfortable. It necessitates understanding the nuances of the status quo, identifying its flaws, and proposing viable alternatives. It is not about mindless rebellion but about informed dissent, driven by a deep-seated desire for a better, more just society. This informed dissent requires careful consideration of the complexities of the issues at hand, a willingness to listen to opposing viewpoints, and a commitment to evidence-based reasoning. It is not enough to simply disagree; one must also be able to articulate a well-reasoned argument and propose a constructive alternative.

To further complicate matters, the line between sanity and madness is often blurred, particularly when viewed through the lens of societal norms. What is considered "normal" can vary drastically across cultures and time periods. The individual who challenges these norms may be perceived as insane, even if their ideas are ultimately beneficial to society. Therefore, it is crucial to cultivate a sense of empathy and understanding towards those who are different, to recognize that their perspectives may offer valuable insights that would otherwise be missed. This requires a willingness to challenge our own biases and assumptions, to step outside of our comfort zones, and to engage in open and honest dialogue with those who hold different beliefs.

I need you to understand that the "Lunatic's Guide to Sanity" also implies a need for self-acceptance. Embracing one's own unique perspective, quirks, and imperfections is an essential step towards genuine sanity. It means rejecting the pressure to conform to unrealistic ideals and celebrating the diversity of human experience. This self-acceptance allows individuals to develop a strong sense of self-worth, which in turn empowers them to challenge the status quo and advocate for their beliefs. It is a foundation upon which one can build a life of purpose and meaning, a life that is not dictated by the expectations of others but by one's own authentic values.

Through the idea of "The Lunatic's Guide to Sanity" I intend to propose a radical shift in perspective, urging us to reconsider the value of conformity and embrace the power of nonconformity. I want to celebrate the courage of those who dare to question, to challenge, and to dissent, recognizing that true progress often stems from the margins, from the voices of the outsiders who refuse to be silenced.

By embracing the perspective of the "lunatic," by daring to question the status quo, we can unlock the potential for genuine sanity, both individually and collectively, and navigate the complexities of a world in crisis with clarity, courage, and an unwavering commitment to truth and justice. Only then can we hope to build a society that is not only more just but also more resilient, more creative, and truly more sane, a society that values diversity of thought and celebrates the contributions of all its members, regardless of their conformity to established norms. This requires a continuous process of self-reflection, critical thinking, and a constant willingness to challenge our own assumptions and biases, ensuring that we remain open to new perspectives and committed to the pursuit of truth and justice.

THE IMPORTANCE OF CIVIC ENGAGEMENT

The preceding discussion explored the crucial role of technology in both undermining and bolstering democratic systems. We saw how the digital divide, a stark chasm separating those with access to information and those without, profoundly impacts the ability of citizens to engage meaningfully in the political process. But even with equal access to technology and information, the fight for a thriving democracy requires something more fundamental: active, engaged citizenship. The health of any democracy rests not solely on its technological infrastructure, but on the unwavering commitment of its citizens to participate actively in shaping their governance and holding their leaders accountable. This active participation, what we term civic engagement, is the lifeblood of a truly representative and responsive government.

Civic engagement encompasses a wide spectrum of activities, ranging from voting in elections – the most basic form of participation – to actively participating in community organizations, advocating for specific policies, and holding elected officials accountable for their actions. It's about more than simply casting a ballot every few years; it's about consistently engaging with the political process, contributing to public discourse, and working collaboratively to solve shared problems. It's about being a vigilant guardian of democratic values, constantly pushing back against the erosion of civil liberties and the concentration of power.

Consider, for example, the success of the Civil Rights Movement in the United States. This wasn't solely the result of legislative action or court decisions; it was fueled by the tireless efforts of countless ordinary citizens who engaged in boycotts, marches, and civil disobedience. Their collective actions, often met with brutal repression, forced the nation to confront its deeply ingrained racial injustices. The movement's success stands as a powerful testament to the transformative potential of organized, grassroots civic engagement. The individuals involved understood that their voice, individually small, could become a powerful roar when joined with others. Their consistent, courageous participation altered the political landscape irrevocably, leaving an enduring legacy of progress and demonstrating that even systemic injustice can be challenged and overcome through sustained civic action.

Similarly, the women's suffrage movement, spanning decades of tireless campaigning and advocacy, ultimately secured the right to vote for women in many countries around the world. This wasn't a spontaneous event; it was the result of decades of dedicated effort by women who challenged societal norms, organized protests, and lobbied tirelessly for legislative change. Their unwavering commitment to their cause serves as a prime example of how sustained civic engagement can lead to profound social change, significantly altering power dynamics and expanding democratic participation.

The power of civic engagement is not limited to large-scale movements. It manifests in myriad everyday actions, each contributing to the overall health of a democratic society. Volunteering at a local soup kitchen, participating in a neighborhood watch program, attending town hall meetings, contacting elected officials to express concerns or support, or simply engaging in respectful dialogue with those who hold differing viewpoints—all of these actions represent valuable forms of civic engagement. These actions, though seemingly small in isolation, collectively weave the fabric of a vibrant and responsive democracy. They signal to the governing powers that the citizenry remains informed, engaged, and ready to hold them accountable for their decisions.

However, the path of civic engagement often requires overcoming significant obstacles, including apathy, cynicism, and feelings of powerlessness. In many societies, particularly those marked by deep-seated inequality or political polarization, individuals may feel alienated from the political process, believing that their voice does not matter or that their participation will not make a difference. This sense of disengagement is a serious threat to democratic governance, leaving space for powerful entities to manipulate the system for their own benefit.

Combating this apathy requires a concerted effort to foster a culture of civic participation from a young age. Education plays a crucial role, teaching young people about their rights and responsibilities as citizens, promoting critical thinking skills, and encouraging them to actively participate in their communities. In addition, educational systems must move beyond rote memorization of facts and figures, fostering engagement through active learning, including simulation exercises, mock debates, and community service projects. These activities instill a deeper sense of civic responsibility and cultivate the skills necessary for active participation in democratic processes.

Media has a vital role to play in promoting civic engagement. By providing accurate and unbiased information, fostering robust public discourse, and holding elected officials accountable, media outlets can contribute significantly to an informed and engaged citizenry. However, the proliferation of misinformation and the erosion of trust in traditional media outlets present significant challenges. It is imperative that media organizations commit to upholding journalistic ethics and combatting the spread of disinformation. Transparency, fact-checking, and the promotion of media literacy are crucial steps in rebuilding trust and ensuring an informed public.

Beyond formal education and media, various community organizations and initiatives can play a significant role in fostering civic engagement. These include non-profit organizations, faith-based groups, and community centers that provide opportunities for individuals to connect with others, learn new skills, and participate in collective action. Such organizations can serve as hubs for civic engagement, offering platforms for dialogue, community organizing, and advocacy. They can also provide valuable training and resources to help individuals become more effective advocates for change.

Ultimately, strengthening democracy requires a fundamental shift in mindset — a move away from passive spectatorship to active engagement. It requires a commitment to lifelong learning, a willingness to engage in respectful dialogue with those who hold differing viewpoints, and a determination to hold our elected officials accountable for their actions. It is a continuous process, one that demands consistent vigilance and dedication, and requires challenging comfortable narratives and established power structures. The responsibility for rebuilding trust and strengthening democratic institutions lies not solely with government officials but with each and every citizen. By embracing our civic duty and actively participating in the affairs of our communities, we can collectively safeguard the foundations of democracy and create a more just and equitable society. The alternative – disengagement and apathy – paves the path for the erosion of democratic values and the rise of authoritarianism. The choice, therefore, is clear: engage, or risk losing the very freedoms we hold dear.

STRENGTHENING INDEPENDENT INSTITUTIONS

The fight for a robust democracy extends beyond individual vigilance and critical thinking; it necessitates the unwavering strength and independence of vital institutions. A healthy democracy isn't merely a collection of informed citizens; it's a system of checks and balances, where independent institutions act as guardians against the encroachment of power, ensuring fairness, accountability, and transparency. These institutions – the judiciary, a free press, and vibrant civil society organizations – are the pillars upon which a truly democratic society rests. Their erosion signifies a creeping authoritarianism, a subtle shift towards a system where the powerful dictate, rather than serve, the people.

The judiciary, the cornerstone of the rule of law, must operate free from political manipulation. Judges must be appointed based on merit, not political affiliation, and must be empowered to make impartial judgments, irrespective of external pressure. The independence of the judiciary is not merely a procedural matter; it's the very essence of justice. When courts are subject to political interference, the scales of justice are tipped, undermining the public's faith in the legal system and fostering a climate of impunity for those in power. This erosion of trust can lead to widespread disillusionment, encouraging citizens to turn away from legal recourse and potentially resort to extra-legal means of redress. Cases where judges are openly harassed, threatened, or even imprisoned for delivering unpopular verdicts paint a stark picture of a democracy in decline. This isn't confined to developing nations;

even in established democracies, subtle pressures – through political appointments, funding cuts, or public vilification – can undermine the judiciary's ability to function impartially. A robust judiciary requires not only independent judges but also transparent processes, accessible legal aid, and protection mechanisms for those who dare to challenge powerful interests. The appointment process itself must be rigorously scrutinized, with clear criteria and mechanisms for public input, to prevent political capture.

A free and independent press plays a crucial role in holding those in power accountable. Journalists serve as the watchdogs of society, investigating corruption, exposing wrongdoing, and providing the public with the information necessary to make informed decisions. A vibrant press is not just about delivering news; it's about investigative journalism, holding power accountable through rigorous scrutiny. The ability of journalists to operate without fear of censorship, intimidation, or reprisal is paramount. Unfortunately, in many parts of the world, journalists are routinely silenced, imprisoned, or even killed for their work. This chilling effect on freedom of expression creates a climate of fear, where truth is suppressed, and the public is kept in the dark. The digital age has presented both challenges and opportunities for investigative journalism. The internet offers unprecedented opportunities for reaching audiences, but it also presents challenges in terms of disinformation, online harassment, and the spread of unsubstantiated claims. Protecting journalists requires not only legal safeguards but also a commitment from society to value their role and support their work. This includes advocating for the safety of journalists, challenging censorship, and supporting independent media outlets financially and through public awareness campaigns.

Civil society organizations, encompassing a broad spectrum of non-governmental groups, from human rights organizations to environmental advocacy groups, play a critical role in holding governments and corporations accountable. They serve as vital voices in promoting human rights, defending vulnerable populations, and advancing social justice. Independent civil society organizations act as a counterbalance to state power, advocating for policy changes, mobilizing public opinion, and providing essential services. However, these organizations often face significant challenges, including restrictions on their activities, funding cuts, legal harassment, and even outright violence. Their ability to operate freely is vital for a healthy democracy, as they serve as a crucial bridge between the public and the government. They represent the interests of diverse groups and play a vital role in holding power accountable. The increasing scrutiny and regulation of civil society organizations often stem from a desire to control or silence dissent, a dangerous trend that undermines the foundational principles of a free and open society. Strengthening these organizations requires not only legal protection and funding but also public support and a commitment to the values they represent.

Strengthening these independent institutions requires a multi-faceted approach. It necessitates legal reforms to protect these institutions from political interference, ensuring transparency in their operations and preventing undue influence. It also requires increased funding for these institutions, particularly those focused on investigative journalism and human rights, to enable them to effectively carry out their crucial roles. Public awareness campaigns can play a vital role in promoting the importance of these institutions and highlighting the threats they face. Educating the public about the vital role of a free press, an independent judiciary, and strong civil society organizations is crucial in fostering a citizenry that values and protects these institutions.

Additionally, international cooperation plays a crucial role in supporting and strengthening democratic institutions globally. International organizations and governments can provide financial and technical assistance to countries seeking to reform their judicial systems, protect freedom of the press, and promote civil society. Sharing best practices, providing technical expertise, and offering training programs can greatly enhance the capacity of these institutions to function effectively and independently. International pressure can also serve as a deterrent against governments seeking to undermine democratic norms. This international collaboration is essential, as the erosion of democratic institutions in one country can have ripple effects across the globe.

The fight for a vigorous and thriving democracy requires a continuous commitment to strengthening independent institutions. It is a battle fought not only in courtrooms and legislatures but also in the public square, in the newsrooms, and in the hearts and minds of citizens. By understanding the vital role these institutions play and actively working to protect their independence and integrity, we can safeguard the future of democracy, ensuring a fairer, more just, and accountable society for all. Ignoring these threats is to surrender the fight, allowing the slow erosion of freedom to continue unchallenged, leaving us vulnerable to the whims of unchecked power. The preservation of democratic values necessitates constant vigilance and an unwavering commitment to the principles of justice, freedom of expression, and accountability. The struggle is ongoing, demanding sustained effort and collaboration from citizens, institutions, and the international community. Only through such collective action can we hope to safeguard the hard-won liberties that define a truly democratic society.

GLOBAL COOPERATION AND SOLIDARITY

The erosion of trust within national borders, as discussed previously, is a serious threat to democratic stability. However, the challenges facing democracy are not confined to individual nations. The interconnected nature of the modern world means that threats to democracy in one country often have ripple effects globally. Authoritarianism, misinformation campaigns, and economic inequality frequently transcend national boundaries, demanding a concerted, international response. This necessitates a re-evaluation of global cooperation and solidarity as crucial tools in defending democratic values and human rights worldwide.

International organizations, such as the United Nations, the Organization for Security and Co-operation in Europe (OSCE), and regional bodies like the European Union, play a vital role in fostering cooperation and coordinating efforts to protect democracy. The UN, with its broad mandate encompassing peace and security, human rights, and development, serves as a platform for dialogue, diplomacy, and the establishment of international norms and standards. The Universal Declaration of Human Rights, a cornerstone of international human rights law, provides a framework for protecting fundamental freedoms and holding states accountable for their human rights records. However, the effectiveness of these organizations is often hampered by the inherent complexities of international relations, the power dynamics between states, and the limitations of their mandates and resources.

The OSCE, for instance, has a specific focus on promoting democracy, human rights, and the rule of law in its member states. Its monitoring missions, election observation efforts, and conflict prevention initiatives have played a significant role in supporting democratic transitions and preventing the escalation of conflicts. However, the OSCE's effectiveness can be significantly undermined by the lack of consensus among its diverse membership, often reflecting geopolitical tensions and differing interpretations of democratic principles.

The European Union, with its robust institutional framework and commitment to the rule of law, has also been at the forefront of promoting democratic values in its member states and beyond. Its enlargement process has been instrumental in supporting the transition to democracy in several Eastern European countries, though challenges remain. The EU's engagement with its neighboring countries, through its Eastern Partnership, also aims to foster democracy and good governance. However, the EU's own internal challenges, coupled with growing Euroscepticism, have hampered its ability to project its democratic values as effectively as in previous years.

Beyond formal international organizations, civil society plays a critical role in promoting global cooperation and solidarity for democracy. Transnational networks of human rights defenders, journalists, and activists work tirelessly to document human rights abuses, expose authoritarian regimes, and advocate for democratic reforms. Their work, often carried out in the face of significant risks, provides a vital counterbalance to state power and sheds light on issues that might otherwise remain hidden.

However, even the most effective international mechanisms are subject to limitations. The principle of state sovereignty, while crucial for the international order, can sometimes shield authoritarian regimes from external scrutiny and intervention. The lack of effective enforcement mechanisms for international law often allows human rights violations to go unpunished. Geopolitical considerations and national interests frequently outweigh considerations of human rights and democratic values, as witnessed in various instances of selective enforcement of international norms.

The successes of global cooperation in defending democracy are demonstrable. International pressure has successfully led to the release of political prisoners, the investigation of human rights abuses, and the implementation of democratic reforms in several countries. The establishment of international criminal tribunals, such as the International Criminal Court, has contributed to the fight against impunity for war crimes and crimes against humanity. International election observation missions have helped ensure free and fair elections in numerous countries, fostering democratic processes.

Yet, the failures are equally, if not more, significant. The international community's response to the rise of authoritarianism in several countries has been often hesitant and ineffective. The failure to prevent or adequately address humanitarian crises and armed conflicts often undermines democratic institutions and exacerbates human rights violations. The lack of effective coordination and resource mobilization among international actors hampers efforts to address global challenges to democracy. The rise of populist and nationalist movements, often characterized by anti-globalist sentiment, further weakens international cooperation mechanisms.

Strengthening global cooperation and solidarity requires a multi-pronged approach. First, international organizations need to be reformed to enhance their effectiveness and accountability. This includes strengthening their mandates, improving their resource mobilization capacities, and ensuring greater transparency and inclusiveness in their decision-making processes. Second, states need to demonstrate a greater commitment to upholding international law and respecting human rights. This includes ratifying and implementing international treaties, cooperating with international investigations, and holding perpetrators of human rights abuses accountable.

Third, civil society organizations need to be empowered to play a more active role in promoting democracy and human rights globally. This requires providing them with greater protection from repression, ensuring their access to funding, and facilitating collaboration among them. Finally, the international community needs to develop more effective mechanisms for addressing the root causes of democratic backsliding. This includes combating corruption, promoting good governance, supporting independent media, strengthening civil society, and ensuring economic justice.

The future of democracy depends in large part on our ability to forge a stronger global consensus on the importance of democratic values and human rights. This requires a renewed commitment to international cooperation and solidarity, based on a shared understanding of the threats to democracy and the collective responsibility to defend it. The challenges are significant, but the stakes are even higher. The alternative — a world characterized by unchecked authoritarianism and human rights abuses — is simply unacceptable. Building a more just and democratic world demands not only national efforts but a global, collaborative endeavor. The time for decisive action is now.

THE MORAL IMPERATIVE TO RESIST

THE ETHICAL DIMENSION OF DISSENT

The preceding discussion highlighted the urgent need for global cooperation in defending democratic values, underscoring the interconnectedness of threats to freedom worldwide. However, the fight for democracy is not merely a matter of international diplomacy and institutional reform; it is fundamentally an ethical struggle. This section delves into the ethical dimensions of dissent, exploring the moral imperative to resist injustice and examining the philosophical underpinnings of civil disobedience.

The act of dissent, of challenging established power structures, often carries significant personal risk. Individuals who speak truth to power frequently face social ostracization, economic hardship, imprisonment, or even violence. Yet, the ethical justification for dissent lies in the very foundations of morality itself. Many philosophical traditions posit that individuals possess inherent rights and dignity, and that these rights are not contingent upon the approval of those in power. When a government or other authority violates these fundamental rights, individuals have a moral obligation to resist.

One influential ethical framework for understanding dissent is deontology, which emphasizes duty and moral rules. Deontological ethics, often associated with Immanuel Kant, argues that certain actions are inherently right or wrong, regardless of their consequences. From a deontological perspective, dissent might be seen as a moral duty when the state infringes upon fundamental rights like freedom of speech or assembly. The act of resisting injustice, regardless of the outcome, is considered morally right because it upholds the inherent dignity of individuals and the principles of justice. The potential repercussions – imprisonment, social stigma, or economic ruin – do not diminish the moral obligation to act. Indeed, the willingness to bear these consequences can be seen as a testament to one's commitment to moral principles.

Conversely, consequentialist ethics, exemplified by utilitarianism, judges the morality of an action based on its consequences. A utilitarian approach to dissent would weigh the potential benefits of resisting injustice against the potential harms. If the potential positive outcomes – such as preventing human rights abuses or promoting social justice – outweigh the negative consequences, then dissent is ethically justified. This framework necessitates a careful assessment of the likely impact of different courses of action. For instance, a planned protest may need to consider the potential for violence or disruption, weighing these factors against the potential for positive change. The decision to engage in dissent, therefore, is a calculated risk, demanding a pragmatic and informed assessment of the potential outcomes.

Virtue ethics, another influential ethical framework, focuses on the character of the moral agent rather than specific rules or consequences. This approach emphasizes the importance of cultivating virtues such as courage, justice, and integrity. From this perspective, dissent is not simply a matter of following rules or calculating outcomes; it is a demonstration of moral character. Individuals who actively resist injustice, even in the face of adversity, are displaying moral courage and a commitment to ethical principles. This emphasis on character underscores the personal transformation that accompanies acts of dissent; those who choose to speak truth to power often undergo a profound change, developing a deeper sense of self-awareness and moral conviction.

The ethical considerations surrounding dissent are further complicated by the concept of civil disobedience. Civil disobedience, as defined by Mahatma Gandhi and Martin Luther King Jr., involves the deliberate violation of unjust laws in a non-violent manner. This form of protest explicitly challenges the authority of the state, but does so by adhering to a strict code of non-violent resistance. The ethical justification for civil disobedience lies in its commitment to peaceful change and its adherence to a higher moral law. When laws themselves are unjust, individuals may have a moral obligation to disobey them, provided their actions are non-violent and aim to bring about a more just society.

The challenge lies in distinguishing between justified dissent and actions that are morally reprehensible. Violence, hatred, and the intentional infliction of harm are never justified in the pursuit of political or social change. The ethical imperative to resist injustice must always be tempered by a commitment to non-violent means and a respect for human dignity, even for those who disagree. The line between legitimate protest and violent extremism is crucial, demanding careful discernment and a commitment to peaceful resolution. The history of social movements is fraught with examples of both successful non-violent resistance and tragically violent responses, emphasizing the paramount importance of ethical conduct in the struggle for justice.

The ethical dimensions of dissent extend beyond the individual level. Collective action, such as widespread protests or civil disobedience campaigns, requires collective ethical judgment. The coordination and organization of such movements demand shared values and a commitment to non-violent means. The ethical responsibility extends to the organizers and participants alike, ensuring that actions are strategically planned, well-organized, and executed in a manner that minimizes harm and maximizes impact. The collective nature of dissent requires a high degree of ethical responsibility, given the potential for unintended consequences when many individuals act in concert.

Furthermore, the ethical considerations surrounding dissent must account for the potential for unintended consequences. Even well-intentioned acts of resistance can have unforeseen and negative outcomes. The ethical decision-making process therefore requires careful consideration of all potential impacts, both positive and negative. The assessment of these potential consequences demands both a pragmatic understanding of social dynamics and a firm commitment to ethical principles, ensuring that the pursuit of justice is not pursued at the expense of other ethical considerations. The ethical decision-maker must strive to balance the potential benefits of dissent against the potential risks, seeking to minimize harm while maximizing the positive impact on society.

The ethical imperative to resist injustice is a central theme in the ongoing struggle for democracy and human rights. Whether framed through deontological, consequentialist, or virtue ethics perspectives, the act of dissent is often a morally necessary act when facing authoritarianism or other forms of oppression. However, this imperative must always be tempered by a strict adherence to non-violent means and a careful consideration of the potential consequences. The ethical dimensions of dissent extend beyond individual actions, demanding collective responsibility and a commitment to peaceful, constructive change. Ultimately, the moral justification for resistance lies in the fundamental belief in the inherent dignity and rights of all individuals, and the unwavering commitment to a more just and equitable society. The ongoing struggle for justice is a continual ethical challenge, demanding careful reflection, responsible action, and an unwavering dedication to the principles of non-violence and human rights.

THE PERSONAL COSTS AND REWARDS OF RESISTANCE

The ethical imperative to resist, as explored previously, carries profound implications for individuals who choose to challenge established power structures. This decision, however noble, is rarely without significant personal cost. History is replete with examples of dissidents facing imprisonment, persecution, financial ruin, and social ostracism. The price of speaking truth to power can be steep, ranging from subtle forms of marginalization to outright physical danger. For whistleblowers exposing corporate malfeasance, the consequences can manifest as career destruction, legal battles, and relentless smear campaigns designed to discredit their credibility and silence their voices. Activists challenging oppressive regimes often endure harsher realities: arbitrary detention, torture, disappearance, and even assassination. The personal sacrifices made by these individuals are a testament to their unwavering commitment to justice and their conviction that the truth, however dangerous to speak, must be told.

The distressing effect of potential repercussions often prevents individuals from speaking out, perpetuating cycles of injustice and silencing dissent. The fear of losing one's job, facing social isolation, or becoming a target of harassment can be paralyzing. This fear is often deliberately cultivated by those in power, who seek to maintain control through intimidation and repression. Propaganda campaigns, carefully crafted to demonize dissenters and portray them as threats to societal stability, further exacerbate this climate of fear. The psychological toll of living under such conditions can be significant, contributing to a sense of powerlessness and despair. This pervasive atmosphere of fear, intentionally fostered by authoritarian regimes, serves to effectively suppress opposition and maintain the status quo. The normalization of silence, born out of fear and intimidation, allows injustice to thrive.

Yet, the personal costs of resistance are not solely defined by suffering and hardship. While the risks are undeniably real and often severe, they are counterbalanced by profound personal rewards. For many dissidents, the act of standing up against injustice is itself a source of immense strength and fulfillment. The knowledge that they have acted according to their conscience, that they have chosen principle over self-preservation, can provide a deep sense of purpose and meaning. This inner conviction, this unwavering belief in the righteousness of their cause, is often a powerful source of resilience, enabling them to withstand immense pressure and adversity. The act of defying oppression, of refusing to be complicit in injustice, is often a deeply transformative experience, leading to personal growth and a strengthened sense of self.

The collective nature of resistance can provide a powerful source of support and solidarity. Dissidents often find strength and encouragement in community, forging bonds of friendship and mutual support with like-minded individuals. These connections provide a vital buffer against isolation and despair, reinforcing the belief that they are not alone in their struggle. The shared experience of resistance creates a powerful sense of belonging and camaraderie, fostering resilience and promoting collective action. This collective action, in turn, can amplify the impact of individual acts of resistance, creating a ripple effect that expands the movement's reach and influence.

The impact of resistance extends far beyond the individual. The courageous acts of dissidents often inspire others to speak out, igniting movements for social change and contributing to broader societal shifts towards greater justice and equality. The seemingly small acts of defiance—a single protest sign, a whispered truth, a refusal to comply—can accumulate, creating a wave of resistance that eventually overpowers oppression. Consider the impact of individuals like Nelson Mandela, whose unwavering resistance to apartheid inspired millions and ultimately contributed to the dismantling of that oppressive system. Or think of the countless activists who fought for women's suffrage, their persistent efforts eventually leading to legal recognition of women's rights. These examples underscore the profound societal impact that can result from individual acts of courage.

The rewards of resistance are not always immediate or easily discernible. The fight for justice is often a long and arduous struggle, characterized by setbacks, disappointments, and periods of intense hardship. The outcomes of resistance are rarely guaranteed; the path to meaningful change is often fraught with uncertainty and requires sustained commitment over extended periods. Yet, the potential for positive impact, both on the personal and societal levels, justifies the personal risks involved. The knowledge that one's actions contribute to a better future, however indirectly, can be a powerful motivator, offering sustenance during challenging moments.

Furthermore, the long-term effects of resistance are often underestimated. The legacy of those who have bravely challenged injustice can inspire future generations to fight for what is right. Their stories serve as reminders of the importance of courage, perseverance, and the enduring power of human agency in the face of oppression. The narratives of dissent, passed down through generations, become symbols of hope and resistance, offering strength and inspiration to those who may one day face similar challenges. This legacy of resistance is an invaluable inheritance, shaping moral landscapes and empowering individuals to challenge injustice in the future.

It is crucial to acknowledge the complexities of resistance. Not all acts of dissent are equally effective or ethically justifiable.

The methods employed, the targets chosen, and the wider context all play a crucial role in determining the overall impact of any resistance movement. A nuanced understanding of power dynamics, the interplay of social and political forces, and the potential for unintended consequences is essential for creating effective and ethical strategies for social change. Careful planning, strategic alliances, and a commitment to non-violent methods are critical for maximizing the positive impact and minimizing the risks of resistance. The journey towards justice requires both courage and wisdom.

In conclusion, the personal costs and rewards of resistance are inextricably linked. While the risks are undeniable and often substantial, the potential for profound personal growth, societal impact, and the creation of a more just world outweigh the challenges. The narrative of resistance is not merely one of suffering and sacrifice; it is a story of courage, resilience, and the enduring human capacity to challenge injustice and fight for a better future. The legacy of those who have bravely spoken truth to power serves as a powerful reminder of the moral imperative to resist and the transformative power of individual and collective action. The fight for justice is an ongoing struggle, demanding sustained commitment, careful planning, and an unwavering belief in the inherent dignity and rights of all people. The personal journey of resistance, while arduous, is ultimately a journey towards a more just and equitable world, one in which the voices of dissent are not silenced, but amplified and heard.

FINDING STRENGTH IN SOLIDARITY

The solitary act of resistance, however courageous, often feels like a pebble thrown into a vast ocean. Its impact, while potentially significant in its own right, can be dwarfed by the collective force of a coordinated movement. This is where the power of solidarity emerges as a crucial element in the fight against injustice. Finding strength in numbers, in shared purpose and mutual support, transforms isolated acts of defiance into a powerful wave capable of reshaping the political landscape.

Solidarity isn't simply about being part of a large group; it's about forging genuine connections, building trust, and creating a network of mutual support. It's about recognizing that the struggle for justice is a collective endeavor, requiring shared strategies, resource pooling, and a commitment to collective well-being. This interconnectedness provides resilience against the inevitable setbacks and challenges inherent in any resistance movement. When one individual falters, the collective strength of the network can provide the necessary support to prevent collapse. When one voice is silenced, others rise up to amplify the message, ensuring that the struggle continues unabated.

The history of social movements is replete with examples of the power of solidarity. The American Civil Rights Movement, for instance, wasn't built solely on the charismatic leadership of Martin Luther King Jr. It was the combined efforts of countless individuals, from ordinary citizens to prominent figures, working together, often at great personal risk, to challenge the deeply ingrained system of racial segregation. The sit-ins, marches, and boycotts were only effective because of the widespread participation and unwavering commitment of a unified movement. The courage of one individual was multiplied exponentially by the collective strength of thousands, creating a force that ultimately forced the nation to confront its own history of racial injustice.

Similarly, the anti-apartheid movement in South Africa demonstrated the extraordinary power of international solidarity. The global condemnation of apartheid, fueled by the unwavering resistance of South African activists and the concerted efforts of international organizations and governments, played a pivotal role in bringing an end to that oppressive regime. The movement transcended geographical boundaries, uniting people from all walks of life in a shared commitment to ending racial discrimination. This global network of support provided essential resources, amplified the voices of South African activists, and exerted significant pressure on the apartheid government, ultimately contributing to its downfall.

The success of these, and countless other movements, is not just a testament to the power of numbers, but also to the effectiveness of strategic collaboration. Solidarity networks provide a platform for sharing information, coordinating actions, and developing strategies that maximize impact while minimizing risk. They allow for the pooling of resources, expertise, and skills, enabling movements to overcome logistical challenges and sustain their efforts over extended periods. The collective intelligence of a diverse group of individuals can generate creative solutions and effective strategies that might not be possible for isolated individuals working alone.

Solidarity networks offer vital emotional and psychological support. The struggle for social change can be intensely demanding, both physically and emotionally. The constant threat of reprisal, the burden of responsibility, and the weariness of protracted struggle can take a heavy toll on activists and dissidents. Solidarity provides a buffer against isolation and despair, offering a sense of belonging, mutual encouragement, and shared purpose. The shared experience of resistance creates strong bonds of camaraderie and mutual respect, strengthening resolve and fostering resilience in the face of adversity.

The importance of building strong solidarity networks extends beyond the immediate context of resistance movements. It's essential for the long-term sustainability and effectiveness of any effort to challenge injustice. A strong network provides a foundation for future activism, enabling movements to adapt to changing circumstances, recruit new members, and maintain momentum over time. It ensures the continuity of the struggle, preserving the legacy of past struggles and inspiring future generations to carry the torch.

However, building effective solidarity networks requires careful consideration of several factors. The diversity of perspectives and experiences within a movement can be both a source of strength and a potential source of conflict. Navigating these complexities requires a commitment to inclusive dialogue, respectful disagreement, and collaborative decision-making. Clear communication, shared goals, and a commitment to transparency are essential for maintaining trust and ensuring that the collective effort remains focused on the overarching objective.

Also, the security of individuals within a solidarity network is paramount. Sharing information and coordinating actions can expose members to increased risk. It's crucial to develop strategies to mitigate these risks, protecting the identity and safety of activists and ensuring that information is shared responsibly and securely. This requires a high degree of trust and a shared commitment to collective security.

The fight for justice is a collective journey, demanding collaboration, mutual support, and unwavering commitment. Solidarity empowers individuals to overcome the limitations of individual action, creating a collective force that is far greater than the sum of its parts. It provides the strength to resist oppression, the resilience to withstand adversity, and the hope to create a more just and equitable world. Building strong solidarity networks is not just a tactical necessity; it's a moral imperative, a testament to the power of shared humanity and the enduring human capacity for collective action in the face of injustice. The history of successful resistance movements underscores the crucial role of solidarity in achieving meaningful social change. It is in these networks of mutual support and shared struggle that true power resides, and from which the most profound and lasting transformations emerge. The future of justice rests on our ability to forge, strengthen, and sustain these vital connections.

HOPE IN ADVERSITY

The Long Arc of Justice

The fight for justice rarely unfolds in a neat, easily digestible timeline. It's often a grueling ultra-marathon across treacherous terrain. Setbacks are inevitable, moments of profound discouragement frequent. The weight of systemic oppression can feel insurmountable, the opposition seemingly monolithic and invincible. The temptation to succumb to despair, to abandon the struggle, is a constant companion. Yet, it is precisely in these moments of deepest darkness that the unwavering commitment to the moral imperative to resist is most critically tested. It is in these moments that hope, fragile as it may seem, becomes the essential fuel that keeps the flame of resistance burning.

Maintaining hope in the face of relentless adversity requires a deep understanding of the nature of systemic change. It's not a linear progression, a smooth upward trajectory from oppression to liberation. Rather, it's a messy, chaotic process, characterized by fits and starts, punctuated by victories, large and small, and setbacks equally significant. Understanding this inherent unpredictability is crucial to cultivating resilience. Expecting smooth sailing only sets us up for disillusionment and defeat when the inevitable storms arise. The long arc of justice, to borrow from Dr. Martin Luther King Jr., bends toward justice, but it bends slowly, and with considerable effort.

The history of social movements is replete with examples of protracted struggles, where the path to victory was paved with years, even decades, of persistent activism. The women's suffrage movement, for instance, wasn't a quick and easy win. It took decades of tireless campaigning, lobbying, protesting, and countless acts of individual and collective defiance to secure the right to vote for women in many countries. The fight for LGBTQ+ rights, similarly, demonstrates the long-haul nature of social change. Each incremental gain, from the decriminalization of homosexuality to marriage equality, was the result of protracted struggles, often marked by periods of intense backlash and setbacks. These battles, frequently fought across generations, illustrate the significance of sustained engagement and the importance of passing the baton to future generations of activists.

Let's go back and consider the anti-apartheid movement in South Africa. The struggle against apartheid spanned decades, witnessing periods of both intense repression and moments of remarkable progress. The sacrifices made by countless individuals, from Nelson Mandela and his fellow political prisoners to the countless activists who risked their lives protesting the regime, underscore the profound commitment required to achieve lasting change. The international sanctions and boycotts, maintained over years, further demonstrate the sustained pressure necessary to dismantle oppressive systems. This wasn't a quick win; it was a testament to the power of unwavering perseverance in the face of seemingly insurmountable odds.

Similarly, the Civil Rights Movement in the United States showcases the power of sustained, non-violent resistance. The movement's success was not a sudden event but the culmination of years of organized protests, boycotts, and civil disobedience. Each victory, from the desegregation of buses to the passage of the Civil Rights Act, was a building block, a steppingstone on the long road to racial equality. The struggle continues to this day, highlighting the ongoing need for perseverance in the fight against systemic racism.

These historical examples illuminate a crucial aspect of maintaining hope: recognizing that progress often comes incrementally, not in sweeping, revolutionary changes. Each small victory, each legal challenge won, each policy reform implemented, is a step forward, contributing to a larger pattern of change. It's essential to celebrate these successes, to acknowledge the significance of even seemingly minor victories, as they reaffirm the potential for positive change and offer vital sustenance on the long road ahead. These successes provide the morale boost, the evidence that the struggle is not futile, that the tireless efforts are making a difference.

However, acknowledging the incremental nature of progress does not diminish the importance of grand vision and ambitious goals. It is crucial to hold onto the long-term vision, the ultimate objective, even when faced with setbacks. This long-term vision acts as an anchor, providing direction and a sense of purpose when the path forward feels uncertain. It's the compass that guides us through the darkest hours, reminding us of the ultimate goal and providing the strength to continue the fight. Furthermore, maintaining a long-term vision necessitates the development of strategies designed for sustained engagement.

This sustained engagement necessitates an understanding of the importance of self-care and mutual support. The fight for justice is emotionally and physically draining. The constant pressure, the risk of reprisal, and the sheer weight of the struggle can take a toll on individuals, potentially leading to burnout and discouragement. Therefore, fostering a culture of mutual support and self-care is crucial for maintaining resilience within the movement. This means encouraging regular breaks, providing opportunities for rest and reflection, and creating networks of support that offer both emotional and practical assistance. Activist burnout is a real threat, and mitigating it through effective self-care strategies and supportive networks is vital for the long-term success of the movement.

Maintaining hope in the face of adversity requires a deep-seated belief in the inherent goodness of humanity, a belief that even in the darkest hours, the capacity for compassion, empathy and altruism still exists. This belief, grounded in the fundamental human desire for justice and equality, fuels the relentless pursuit of a better world, even when the path is arduous and uncertain. It is this unwavering conviction in the possibility of positive change, that despite all challenges and obstacles, justice can prevail, that allows us to persevere. The fight for justice is a testament to our enduring capacity for hope, a testament to our innate human resilience, our commitment to a better future. It is in holding onto this belief, in nurturing our collective hope, that we find the strength to continue the struggle, to keep moving forward, inching closer towards that distant, but ever-approaching horizon of justice. The journey may be long, arduous and often disheartening, but the destination is worth fighting for. The long arc of justice bends towards justice. Our perseverance ensures it continues to bend.

Passing the Torch

THE NEXT GENERATION OF ACTIVISTS

The fight for a just and equitable society is not a solo endeavor; it's a relay race across generations. The victories we celebrate today are built on the shoulders of those who came before us, and the battles we face tomorrow will require the unwavering commitment of those who follow. Passing the torch – cultivating the next generation of activists – is not merely an act of succession, but a fundamental imperative for the survival and growth of any movement striving for meaningful social change. This isn't simply about training replacements; it's about building a vibrant, diverse, and resilient community of change-makers, capable of adapting to evolving challenges and sustaining the fight for justice across time.

The foundation of this intergenerational transfer of knowledge and commitment lies in education. It's not enough to passively absorb historical narratives; we must actively engage young minds, fostering critical thinking and a deep understanding of the systems of power that perpetuate inequality. This necessitates creating educational programs – both formal and informal – that equip future generations with the tools they need to analyze societal injustices, identify root causes, and develop effective strategies for resistance. These programs should transcend rote memorization and move towards experiential learning, allowing young people to directly engage in the communities they aim to serve and witness firsthand the impact of their work. Field trips to community centers, participation in service projects, and opportunities to meet with and learn from established activists are crucial components of such an approach.

Additionally, the curriculum must be diverse and inclusive, reflecting the multitude of perspectives and experiences within the broader movement. It must grapple with the complexities of intersectionality, recognizing that injustices are often interconnected and impact different communities in unique ways. It's not enough to just understand the history of civil rights; we must equally explore the histories of women's rights, LGBTQ+ rights, environmental justice, disability rights, and other movements for social change. By examining these interconnected struggles, we cultivate an understanding of systemic oppression and the importance of building solidarity across diverse communities. This understanding is essential to building effective coalitions and achieving transformative change. For example, the connections between environmental degradation and its disproportionate impact on marginalized communities can be explored; or how economic inequality reinforces existing social injustices. The goal isn't to simply add more names and dates to a list, but to help students understand the root causes of social injustice and develop critical analysis skills that allow them to understand current struggles within this historical context.

Mentorship is another crucial component of cultivating future activists. The guidance and support of experienced activists can provide invaluable direction and encouragement for young people who are just beginning to find their voice. Such mentorship programs can take many forms, including one-on-one guidance, peer-to-peer learning networks, and workshops or training sessions led by seasoned activists. Mentors can help young people navigate the complexities of activism, providing guidance on strategic planning, communication skills, fundraising, and navigating the potential challenges and risks involved in speaking truth to power.

Beyond formal mentorship programs, fostering intergenerational dialogue and collaboration within activist circles is essential. The wisdom and experience of older generations can complement the fresh perspectives and energy of younger generations, creating a powerful synergy that drives effective action. This can be facilitated through joint projects, collaborative workshops, and informal gatherings that allow for the exchange of ideas and experiences. Such interactions can help bridge the generational gap, fostering mutual respect and understanding. The inclusion of diverse voices - based on age, ethnicity, and social background - within the process ensures that the resulting strategies encompass diverse perspectives and better address the complexities of social justice issues.

The creation of opportunities for young people to actively participate in social justice work is crucial. This doesn't necessarily mean thrusting them immediately into high-stakes situations, but providing avenues for gradually increasing levels of involvement. Young people can start by participating in community service projects, engaging in volunteer work with relevant organizations, or joining youth-led activism groups. These initial experiences provide a valuable entry point, helping them develop their skills, gain confidence, and discover their passion for social change. Gradually, they can take on more responsibility, learning from their mentors and contributing meaningfully to the broader movement. These initial steps, while small, are important building blocks in their overall journey towards social activism.

However, cultivating the next generation of activists is not solely about providing opportunities for engagement; it's about creating a supportive and inclusive environment where young people feel empowered to speak up, to challenge the status quo, and to contribute their unique perspectives to the fight for social justice. This means creating spaces where their voices are not just heard, but valued and actively sought out. Their perspectives, often fresh and uninhibited, can offer valuable insights and innovative strategies, challenging the established norms and pushing the movement forward. We must also acknowledge and address the disproportionate challenges faced by young people from marginalized communities in accessing these opportunities, which may require targeted interventions and support systems to ensure equitable access.

It is vital to recognize that activism is a multifaceted endeavor requiring a diverse skillset. It demands not only passion and conviction but also organizational skills, strategic thinking, communication abilities, and an understanding of the legal and political landscape. Therefore, the nurturing of future activists should include comprehensive training and development programs in these areas. Workshops on effective communication strategies, grant writing and fundraising, legal advocacy, and digital campaigning can empower young people to become more effective agents of change.

Crucially, we must acknowledge that activism is not without risk. Young people need to be prepared for potential backlash, criticism, and even harassment. Providing appropriate training and support in navigating these challenges is essential. This includes equipping them with strategies for handling online abuse, coping with setbacks and disappointment, and building resilience in the face of adversity. Mentors and experienced activists can play a crucial role in helping young people develop the emotional intelligence and resilience necessary to navigate the sometimes turbulent waters of social activism.

It is important to foster a culture of collective responsibility and shared leadership within the movement. Activism should not be viewed as a hierarchical structure, but as a collaborative effort where everyone, regardless of age or experience, has a valuable contribution to make. This collaborative approach encourages innovation, prevents burnout, and ensures the sustainability of the movement across generations. Creating platforms for open dialogue, transparent decision-making, and equal participation will foster this sense of collective ownership and strengthen the movement's resilience.

The struggle for justice is a continuous journey, spanning decades and even centuries. It's a journey that requires not only unwavering dedication from those currently engaged but also a robust pipeline of new voices and perspectives. By investing in the education, mentorship, and active engagement of young people, we ensure that the flame of resistance is not only kept alive, but burns brighter with each passing generation. It's a commitment to a future where the ideals of justice, equality, and freedom continue to inspire and motivate future generations of activists to take up the mantle and continue the fight for a more just and equitable world. It is through this intergenerational collaboration that the long arc of justice will bend towards its ultimate goal, ensuring that the values we cherish are not only preserved, but strengthened and carried forward into a brighter tomorrow.

The Art *of* Critical Thinking

SEEING THROUGH THE "FOG OF WAR"

In an era defined by the relentless deluge of information, much of it deliberately distorted, spun, and weaponized, the ability to think critically is not merely a desirable skill, but a fundamental necessity for navigating the complexities of the modern world. It is the intellectual compass that guides us through the fog of war, allowing us to discern truth from falsehood, reason from rhetoric, and ultimately, empowering us to make informed decisions and participate meaningfully in a democratic society. This essay argues that cultivating critical thinking skills, by understanding cognitive biases, logical fallacies, and source evaluation techniques, is not only a personal imperative but also a crucial element in safeguarding individual autonomy and promoting a just and informed political landscape.

The "fog of war," a concept originally coined to describe the uncertainty and chaos inherent in military operations, aptly captures the contemporary information environment. This fog is deliberately thickened by various actors, from state propagandists seeking to manipulate public opinion to commercial entities vying for market share through deceptive advertising, and even well-intentioned individuals unknowingly spreading misinformation through social media. At the heart of this manipulation lie cognitive biases, inherent tendencies in our thinking that can lead to systematic errors in judgment. Confirmation bias, for instance, predisposes us to seek out and favor information that confirms our existing beliefs, while the bandwagon effect encourages us to adopt opinions simply because they are popular. Anchoring bias, where we rely too heavily on the first piece of information received, and the availability heuristic, which leads us to overestimate the likelihood of events that are easily recalled, further complicate our ability to process information objectively. Recognizing these biases is the first step towards mitigating their influence, allowing us to approach information with a more objective and skeptical lens. This requires a conscious effort to seek out diverse perspectives and actively challenge our own assumptions.

Compounding the effect of cognitive biases are logical fallacies, flawed arguments that may appear persuasive but are ultimately based on unsound reasoning. Ad hominem attacks, which target the person making the argument rather than the argument itself, and straw man fallacies, which misrepresent an opponent's position to make it easier to refute, are just two examples of the rhetorical tricks employed to deceive and manipulate. Appeal to emotion, which attempts to sway an audience by manipulating their feelings rather than presenting logical evidence, and false dilemma, which presents only two options when more exist, are equally insidious. A critical thinker must be adept at identifying these fallacies, dismantling their deceptive facade and exposing the underlying weakness of the argument. This requires careful attention to detail, a willingness to question assumptions, and a commitment to logical consistency. Furthermore, it demands the ability to deconstruct complex arguments into their component parts, identifying the premises, the conclusions, and the logical connections (or lack thereof) between them.

However, identifying biases and fallacies is only half the battle. In a world where information is readily available but often unreliable, the ability to evaluate sources critically is vital. This involves questioning the source's motive, considering its potential biases, and scrutinizing its evidence. Is the source credible? What is its reputation? Does it have a vested interest in promoting a particular viewpoint? Is it a primary source or a secondary source? Peer-reviewed academic research generally carries more weight than a blog post written by an anonymous author. Triangulating information, by comparing it with multiple independent sources, is crucial for verifying its accuracy and identifying potential distortions. Furthermore, discerning between fact and opinion is essential. Facts are verifiable and objective, while opinions are subjective and reflect personal beliefs. Mistaking opinions for facts can lead to significant misunderstandings and ultimately, to the acceptance of misinformation. Recognizing the difference between correlation and causation is also crucial. Just because two things happen together doesn't mean one caused the other. Developing media literacy skills, including understanding how algorithms and social media platforms can amplify biases and spread misinformation, is increasingly important.

Beyond its practical applications, critical thinking is also a deeply philosophical endeavor. It requires a commitment to intellectual honesty and a willingness to challenge one's own assumptions. This involves embracing intellectual humility, acknowledging the limits of one's knowledge, and being open to revising beliefs in light of new evidence. It means being able to say, "I was wrong," and learning from mistakes without defensiveness. Furthermore, critical thinking promotes intellectual autonomy, empowering individuals to think for themselves rather than blindly accepting the pronouncements of authority figures. This autonomy is essential for participating in a democratic society, where citizens must be able to make informed decisions about their political representatives and the policies that govern their lives. It also fosters creativity and innovation, allowing individuals to develop original ideas and solutions by challenging conventional wisdom.

Politically, the cultivation of critical thinking is crucial for resisting propaganda and manipulation. In authoritarian regimes, propaganda is often used to control the population and suppress dissent. However, even in democratic societies, misinformation and disinformation can be used to influence elections and undermine public trust in institutions. The spread of "fake news" and conspiracy theories poses a significant threat to democratic discourse. By fostering critical thinking skills, we can empower citizens to resist these manipulative tactics and hold those in power accountable. A citizenry equipped with critical thinking skills is a bulwark against tyranny, capable of discerning truth from lies and making informed decisions that serve the common good. This also necessitates promoting media literacy education in schools and communities, empowering individuals to navigate the complex information landscape responsibly.

The benefits of critical thinking extend far beyond politics and into all aspects of life. In the workplace, critical thinkers are better equipped to solve problems, make sound judgments, and innovate. In personal relationships, critical thinking can help us to communicate more effectively, resolve conflicts constructively, and avoid being manipulated by others. By analyzing situations objectively, we can make better decisions about our health, finances, and relationships. In essence, critical thinking is a life skill that empowers us to live more fulfilling and meaningful lives.

The art of critical thinking is not merely an academic exercise but a vital skill for navigating the complexities of the modern world. By understanding cognitive biases, identifying logical fallacies, and evaluating sources critically, we can pierce the fog of war and discern truth from falsehood. This, in turn, empowers us to make informed decisions, participate meaningfully in democratic processes, and resist the manipulative power of rhetoric. In a world saturated with misinformation, critical thinking is our most vital weapon, safeguarding individual autonomy and promoting a just and informed political landscape. It is an ongoing practice, a constant questioning and re-evaluation, but it is a practice that is essential for those who wish to navigate the world with clarity and integrity. Furthermore, it is a practice that requires cultivation and encouragement, both individually and collectively, to ensure a more informed, rational, and democratic future for all. We must actively promote critical thinking in our educational systems, our communities, and our political discourse to ensure that future generations are equipped to navigate the challenges and opportunities of an increasingly complex world. The future of democracy, and perhaps even the future of humanity, depends on it.

FINDING YOUR VOICE IN THE WILDERNESS

A PHILOSOPHICAL AND POLITICAL EXPLORATION OF SPEAKING TRUTH TO POWER

The act of speaking truth to power is a timeless and fundamental human endeavor. It's a defiant act, fueled by a desire for justice, equality, and a better world. Yet, it's often a daunting one, leaving individuals feeling isolated and insignificant against the monolithic structures of authority. To speak truth in the wilderness requires courage, conviction, and a strategic understanding of power dynamics. This essay will explore the philosophical and political dimensions of this act, examining the practical strategies that empower individuals to find their voice and challenge authority, even when the path ahead seems barren and unforgiving.

Philosophically, the imperative to speak truth to power stems from a commitment to fundamental moral principles. At the heart of this lies the belief in the inherent dignity and worth of every individual. When power structures perpetuate injustice, inequality, or oppression, they deny that dignity. Speaking truth, therefore, becomes a moral obligation, a refusal to passively accept the status quo. Thinkers like Socrates, who famously chose death over compromising his philosophical convictions, embody this principle. His relentless questioning of Athenian authority, though met with hostility, served as a testament to the power of individual conscience and the importance of challenging established norms, even at great personal cost. Socrates understood that the pursuit of truth, even when unpopular, was essential for the health and progress of society. His legacy continues to inspire those who dare to question authority and speak out against injustice.

Furthermore, the act of speaking truth aligns with the pursuit of justice. Philosophers like John Rawls, with his emphasis on fairness and equality in his "Theory of Justice," provide a framework for understanding the ethical imperative to challenge power structures that systematically disadvantage certain groups. Rawls' concept of the "veil of ignorance," where one imagines designing a society without knowing their own future position within it, highlights the inherent unfairness of systems that benefit the powerful at the expense of the vulnerable. By exposing the flaws and injustices inherent in the system, individuals can contribute to a more equitable and just society. This requires a deep understanding of the ethical considerations involved in challenging authority, acknowledging the potential consequences while remaining committed to upholding moral principles. This commitment extends beyond simply identifying injustice; it demands a proactive effort to dismantle the structures that perpetuate it.

Politically, speaking truth to power necessitates a nuanced understanding of the mechanisms through which power operates. Power isn't simply about wielding authority; it's about control over resources, information, and narratives. Challenging power requires disrupting these control mechanisms. This can manifest in various forms of activism, from grassroots organizing, where communities mobilize to address local issues, to civil disobedience, where individuals intentionally break unjust laws to protest and raise awareness. The Arab Spring, for example, demonstrated the potent force of grassroots movements in challenging authoritarian regimes. While the outcomes were varied and complex, the uprisings showcased the power of ordinary citizens to demand change and hold their leaders accountable.

Building alliances is crucial for amplifying marginalized voices. A single voice in the wilderness can easily be ignored or silenced. However, a chorus of voices united in a common cause becomes a force to be reckoned with. These alliances can transcend social, economic, and political boundaries, bringing together diverse groups with shared values and goals. By pooling resources, sharing knowledge, and coordinating efforts, individuals can create a powerful counter-narrative to the dominant ideology. The LGBTQ+ rights movement, for instance, has achieved significant progress by forging alliances with other social justice groups, demonstrating the power of intersectional solidarity.

The power of storytelling cannot be overstated. Statistics and abstract arguments often fail to resonate with the public in the same way that personal narratives do. By sharing stories of lived experiences, individuals can humanize the issues and connect with audiences on an emotional level. These stories can expose the hidden costs of unjust policies and inspire action by demonstrating the real-world impact of power dynamics. Think of the Civil Rights Movement, where personal testimonies of discrimination and segregation galvanized support and ultimately led to significant legislative changes. The use of television broadcasts to show the brutality faced by peaceful protesters played a crucial role in shifting public opinion and creating pressure for reform.

Nevertheless, speaking truth to power is not without its challenges. Those who challenge the status quo often face hostility, intimidation, and even violence. It's crucial to develop strategies for effective communication, even when facing opposition. This includes learning how to articulate your message clearly and persuasively, understanding your audience, and anticipating potential counterarguments. It also requires emotional resilience, the ability to remain calm and focused in the face of adversity. Activists and whistleblowers often experience personal attacks, professional setbacks, and even legal repercussions for their actions. Developing a strong support network and practicing self-care are essential for maintaining the emotional and mental fortitude needed to persevere.

Ethical considerations are crucial. Civil disobedience, for example, requires careful deliberation and a willingness to accept the consequences of one's actions. It's important to distinguish between legitimate dissent and acts of violence or vandalism. The goal should always be to challenge the system in a way that promotes justice and equality, while upholding ethical principles. The philosophy of nonviolent resistance, as articulated by thinkers like Mahatma Gandhi and Martin Luther King Jr., provides a framework for engaging in civil disobedience in a way that is both morally defensible and strategically effective. By adhering to principles of nonviolence, activists can maintain the moral high ground and appeal to the conscience of those in power.

Moreover, in the digital age, the challenges and opportunities for speaking truth to power have expanded exponentially. The internet and social media provide platforms for rapid dissemination of information and the mobilization of global movements. However, these tools also come with the risk of online harassment, disinformation campaigns, and government surveillance. Navigating this complex digital landscape requires media literacy, critical thinking skills, and a commitment to responsible online engagement. Protecting one's privacy and security online is crucial for activists who face potential threats from those they challenge.

It's important to recognize that speaking truth to power is not always about dramatic confrontations or large-scale protests. It can also involve everyday acts of resistance, such as challenging discriminatory language, advocating for ethical practices in the workplace, or supporting marginalized communities. These seemingly small acts can collectively create a culture of dissent and contribute to broader social change. It's about cultivating a mindset of critical engagement and a willingness to speak out against injustice whenever and wherever it occurs.

Speaking truth to power is a complex and multifaceted endeavor that requires philosophical grounding, political acumen, and unwavering commitment to justice. It's about finding your voice in the wilderness, even when it feels small and insignificant. By embracing different forms of activism, building alliances, harnessing the power of storytelling, navigating the ethical considerations involved, and adapting to the challenges of the digital age, individuals can challenge authority, disrupt unjust systems, and contribute to a more equitable and just world. The act of speaking truth is not just a political strategy; it's a moral imperative, a testament to the enduring power of the human spirit to strive for a better future. It's a reminder that even in the darkest wilderness, a single voice can spark a flame of hope and inspire others to join the chorus of dissent, ultimately illuminating a path towards a more just and compassionate society. The journey may be long and arduous, but the pursuit of truth and justice is a reward in itself, a testament to the power of human agency and the enduring hope for a better tomorrow.

The Courage *to* Stand Alone

MAINTAINING HOPE IN A DARKENING WORLD

The world, at times, can feel like a cavernous space, echoes of injustice bouncing off its walls, amplified by the pervasive shadows of apathy and oppression. Speaking out against these injustices, a moral imperative, is often a solitary act, a courageous stand against a tide that threatens to engulf the individual. Maintaining hope and resilience in such a darkening world, where truth seems malleable and righteousness a distant whisper, becomes a crucial, albeit challenging, endeavor. This essay will explore the philosophical and political dimensions of this struggle, examining the challenges of isolation, the importance of nurturing inner strength, and the enduring power of community and human connection in illuminating the path forward.

The courage to stand alone stems from a profound moral compass, a deeply ingrained sense of justice that refuses to be silenced. This can be informed by various philosophical traditions. Kantian ethics, for example, emphasizes the categorical imperative – the moral obligation to act according to principles that could be applied universally. This provides a robust foundation for challenging injustice, even when faced with societal disapproval. Similarly, Stoicism offers a framework for enduring hardship and maintaining inner peace in the face of external chaos. By focusing on what is within our control – our thoughts and actions – Stoics advocate for resilience and acceptance, equipping individuals to weather the storms of a morally compromised world.

Despite that, ethical considerations are often overshadowed by real-world consequences. Speaking truth to power can lead to ostracization, persecution, and even physical harm. The political climate often exacerbates this isolation. Authoritarian regimes actively suppress dissent, creating a chilling effect that discourages individuals from challenging the status quo. Even in democratic societies, powerful vested interests can employ sophisticated strategies to silence critics and maintain their grip on power. This reality highlights the precariousness of hope; it can be easily eroded by the constant barrage of negativity and the fear of reprisal.

To combat this erosion, self-care becomes not a luxury, but a necessity. It is the act of nourishing the spirit, replenishing the reserves of strength needed to confront injustice. This can take many forms, from engaging in mindful practices like meditation and yoga to simply spending time in nature or pursuing creative outlets. By prioritizing their well-being, individuals are better equipped to navigate the emotional and psychological toll of fighting for what they believe in. This aligns with the ancient Greek concept of *eudaimonia*, often translated as flourishing or living well. By cultivating inner harmony and focusing on virtuous actions, individuals can find meaning and purpose even amidst darkness.

We must acknowledge and be aware that isolation is a weapon used by those in power to demoralize and control dissent. Seeking out like-minded individuals, forming alliances, and participating in collective action provides a crucial counterweight. Communities offer a space for shared experience, mutual support, and the amplification of voices that might otherwise be ignored. This echoes the principles of social contract theory, which suggests that individuals come together to form a society based on shared values and a commitment to collective well-being. By joining forces, individuals can overcome the sense of powerlessness and create a potent force for change.

Ultimately, the enduring value of human connection lies in its capacity to remind us of our shared humanity. Empathy, compassion, and solidarity are powerful antidotes to the cynicism and despair that can pervade a darkening world. Recognizing the dignity and worth of every individual, particularly those who are suffering, fuels the commitment to fight for justice and create a more equitable society. This resonates with the philosophical principles of humanism, which emphasizes the inherent value of human beings and seeks to promote their well-being. By fostering connection and understanding, we can build bridges across divides and create a more hopeful future.

The courage to stand alone against injustice is a testimony to the enduring strength of the human spirit. While the challenges are significant – the threat of isolation, the weight of societal pressure, and the pervasiveness of darkness – hope can be sustained through self-care, the power of community, and the unwavering belief in the value of human connection. By drawing upon philosophical and spiritual traditions that offer guidance and solace, individuals can find the inner resilience to persevere in the face of overwhelming odds. Ultimately, the fight for a more just world is not a solitary battle, but a collective endeavor driven by the unwavering hope that even in the darkest of times, the light of compassion and righteousness can prevail.

The Power *of* Decentralization

RECLAIMING CONTROL OF OUR LIVES

In an age defined by increasing centralization – of power, information, and resources – the call for decentralization resonates with a growing urgency. It is a call to reclaim control, to dismantle the structures that consolidate authority in the hands of a select few, and to build a future where individuals and communities are empowered to shape their own destinies. Decentralization, as both a philosophical principle and a political strategy, offers a potent avenue for resisting authoritarian control and fostering resilient, self-sufficient societies.

At its core, decentralization is the distribution of authority, resources, and decision-making power away from a central node and towards a network of individuals, communities, or smaller entities. This dispersal challenges the inherent vulnerabilities of centralized systems, which are susceptible to single points of failure, manipulation, and control. Philosopher Michel Foucault, in his analysis of power dynamics, highlighted how centralized institutions normalize and enforce conformity, suppressing individual agency and dissent. Decentralization, conversely, seeks to unleash this agency by empowering individuals and communities to act autonomously and responsibly.

One critical area where decentralization holds immense potential is in finance. Traditional centralized banking systems grant immense power to institutions that often operate with opacity and prioritize profit over the needs of individuals and communities. The rise of cryptocurrencies and blockchain technology offers a tantalizing glimpse of a decentralized financial future. These technologies allow for peer-to-peer transactions, bypassing traditional intermediaries and empowering individuals with greater control over their money. While still nascent, the potential of decentralized finance (DeFi) to challenge the dominance of centralized banking and create a more equitable financial system is undeniable.

Similarly, the dominance of a few tech giants in the realm of information and communication presents a significant threat to individual freedom and autonomy. These centralized platforms wield immense power over what information we access, how we communicate, and even how we think. Decentralized social media platforms and open-source software projects offer alternatives that prioritize user privacy, data ownership, and freedom of expression. By moving away from centralized, algorithm-driven platforms and embracing decentralized alternatives, we can regain control over our digital lives and resist the manipulation inherent in centralized control.

Beyond finance and technology, decentralization extends to education and community building. The traditional centralized school system, often criticized for its standardized curriculum and top-down approach, can stifle creativity and critical thinking. Decentralized alternatives, such as homeschooling, unschooling, and community-based learning initiatives, offer a more personalized and empowering educational experience. Moreover, the importance of building strong, localized communities cannot be overstated. By supporting independent businesses, fostering self-sufficiency, and engaging in local politics, we can create resilient communities that are less reliant on centralized systems and more capable of withstanding external pressures.

However, the path to decentralization is not without its challenges. A common critique is that decentralized systems can be inefficient and lack the coordination necessary to address large-scale problems. Furthermore, the transition to a decentralized model requires a significant shift in mindset, as individuals must embrace greater responsibility and autonomy in their decision-making. It also requires a conscious effort to navigate the complexities of building and maintaining decentralized networks, ensuring inclusivity, and preventing the re-emergence of centralized power structures within the system.

Despite these challenges, the potential benefits of decentralization are too profound to ignore. In an increasingly interconnected and complex world, decentralization offers a crucial pathway towards reclaiming control of our lives. By empowering individuals and communities, fostering resilience, and promoting self-sufficiency, decentralization creates the conditions for a more just, equitable, and free society. It is a strategy for resisting authoritarianism, not through violent revolution, but through the gradual erosion of centralized power and the cultivation of vibrant, decentralized networks that are resistant to control and capable of shaping their own futures. The power of decentralization lies not just in dismantling centralized structures, but in building something better in their place: a world where individuals and communities are empowered to thrive, not controlled.

THE LONG GAME

PLANTING SEEDS OF HOPE
For Future Generations
In The Struggle Against Tyranny

The struggle against tyranny, a perennial human endeavor, rarely unfolds as a swift and decisive victory. More often, it is a protracted and arduous campaign, a marathon demanding unwavering commitment and a strategic vision that extends far beyond the immediate horizon. To truly break the chains of oppression, we must adopt "the long game," a philosophy predicated on planting seeds of hope for future generations by investing in education, cultivating critical thinking, preserving core values, and harnessing the enduring power of art and culture.

The cornerstone of any long-term strategy against tyranny lies in **education**. A populace equipped with knowledge and critical thinking skills is far less susceptible to manipulation and propaganda. Tyrants often thrive in environments of ignorance, where misinformation can be readily disseminated and dissent easily silenced. By fostering a culture of inquiry and intellectual curiosity, we empower future generations to discern truth from falsehood and to challenge unjust systems. The Enlightenment, for instance, championed reason and scientific inquiry as tools to dismantle the divine right of kings and usher in an era of individual liberty. Thinkers like Locke and Montesquieu, through their writings, laid the intellectual groundwork for revolutions that would reverberate across the globe for centuries. Their investment in education and the dissemination of knowledge, even in the face of persecution, proved to be a potent weapon against tyranny.

Complementary to education is the **cultivation of critical thinking skills**. It is not enough to simply impart information; we must equip future generations with the ability to analyze, evaluate, and synthesize information independently. This involves fostering skepticism, encouraging debate, and promoting intellectual humility. A critical thinker questions authority, seeks evidence, and considers alternative perspectives. Without these skills, individuals are vulnerable to demagoguery and susceptible to accepting simplistic narratives that often serve the interests of the powerful. The Civil Rights Movement in the United States provides a powerful example. Leaders like Martin Luther King Jr. encouraged critical analysis of the prevailing societal structures and empowered individuals to challenge discriminatory laws and practices through non-violent resistance. This critical self-reflection and commitment to justice, cultivated over decades, ultimately led to significant legislative and social change.

Furthermore, the **preservation of values of freedom and justice** serves as a moral compass guiding future generations in their fight against oppression. These values, enshrined in constitutions, legal codes, and ethical frameworks, represent the collective aspirations of a society striving for a better future. By upholding these ideals, even when faced with adversity, we ensure that the flame of hope continues to burn brightly. The Magna Carta, signed in 1215, serves as a testament to this principle. Though initially limited in scope, its recognition of certain fundamental rights paved the way for the development of constitutional principles that continue to inspire movements for freedom and justice worldwide. Its preservation and reinterpretation across centuries showcase the enduring power of core values in shaping the course of history.

Finally, **art, literature, and music** play a crucial role in inspiring resistance and transmitting cultural values across time. These mediums offer a powerful means of expressing dissent, challenging oppressive ideologies, and fostering a sense of collective identity. From the protest songs of the Vietnam War era to the dissident literature of the Soviet Union, art has consistently served as a vehicle for resistance against tyranny. Think of Alexander Solzhenitsyn's "The Gulag Archipelago," a monumental work of literature that exposed the horrors of the Soviet prison system and contributed significantly to the dismantling of the regime. Similarly, the spirituals sung by enslaved African Americans served as a powerful expression of resistance and coded messages of hope for freedom. The ability of art to touch the human spirit and to transcend temporal boundaries makes it an indispensable tool in the long-term struggle against oppression.

The struggle against tyranny is a long and arduous one requiring a strategic vision that extends beyond the immediate. By embracing "the long game," we can plant seeds of hope for future generations by investing in education, cultivating critical thinking, preserving core values, and harnessing the enduring power of art and culture. These are the seeds of freedom that, nurtured over time, can blossom into a society where justice prevails and the specter of tyranny is finally banished. It is a demanding task, requiring patience, perseverance, and a profound belief in the power of future generations to carry the torch of liberty forward. But the stakes are too high to settle for anything less. The future of freedom depends on our commitment to playing the long game.

THE SANITY OF RESISTANCE

CHOOSING DIGNITY OVER CONFORMITY

The versatile history of humanity, throughout its entire evolution, is created by both insidious conformity and courageous resistance. While the former provides the illusion of stability and acceptance, it often serves to prop up injustice and maintain the status quo. True progress, however, is invariably forged in the crucible of resistance, by those who dare to challenge the prevailing winds, even when branded as "lunatics" for their defiance. The true sanity, as this argument postulates, resides not in blind obedience to a corrupt system, but in the unwavering pursuit of truth, justice, and freedom, even at the cost of societal acceptance. To embrace the label of "lunatic" in such circumstances is not to succumb to madness, but to wear it as a badge of honor, a testament to one's refusal to compromise fundamental principles.

The philosophical grounding for this argument lies in the enduring tension between individual autonomy and societal expectations. Existentialists like Sartre and Camus emphasized the inherent freedom of individuals to define their own essence and create their own meaning in a seemingly absurd world. To conform blindly to a system one perceives as unjust is to abdicate this freedom, to relinquish the very core of one's being. Conversely, resistance, even when perceived as irrational by the majority, is an affirmation of individual agency, a declaration that one refuses to be reduced to a cog in a machine of oppression. This resonates with Kant's categorical imperative, which calls for acting only according to principles that could be universalized. If one believes a system is fundamentally immoral, then resisting it becomes a moral imperative, a duty to uphold the inherent dignity of humanity. Furthermore, thinkers like John Stuart Mill, in *On Liberty*, championed the importance of dissenting opinions as crucial for societal progress. He argued that even if a dissenting opinion is wrong, its challenge forces the majority to re-examine and reaffirm their own beliefs, preventing them from becoming stagnant dogmas.

Politically, the sanity of resistance stems from the understanding that power structures are rarely benevolent. They are often self-serving, perpetuating their own interests and suppressing dissent to maintain control. Conformity in such a context is tacit complicity, a passive endorsement of injustice. History is replete with examples of individuals deemed "mad" or "dangerous" for challenging oppressive regimes: Socrates, condemned for corrupting the youth of Athens; Nelson Mandela, imprisoned for his fight against apartheid; Martin Luther King Jr., vilified for his advocacy of civil rights; and even Galileo Galilei, persecuted for his scientific claims that contradicted the established dogma of the Church. Each of these figures faced intense pressure to conform, to recant their beliefs, and to accept the prevailing narrative. Yet, they chose to resist, even in the face of persecution, believing that truth and justice were worth the price. History has vindicated these "lunatics," recognizing their courage and moral clarity in standing against the tide of injustice. Consider also the suffragettes, who were often ridiculed and even imprisoned for demanding the right to vote. Their actions, deemed radical and even "hysterical" at the time, are now recognized as crucial steps towards gender equality. These examples demonstrate that what is considered "sane" or "rational" is often determined by those in power and used to silence dissenting voices.

The challenge, of course, lies in discerning genuine moral outrage from mere contrarianism. True resistance is not driven by ego or a desire for attention, but by a deep-seated commitment to principles of justice, equality, and freedom. It requires careful consideration, reasoned argument, and a willingness to engage in constructive dialogue, even with those who hold opposing views. It is not about recklessly tearing down existing structures without offering viable alternatives, but about building a more just and equitable society based on shared values. A crucial aspect of responsible resistance is self-reflection. Resistors must constantly examine their own motivations and biases to ensure that their actions are truly aimed at promoting justice and not simply driven by personal grievances or ideological dogmatism. The line between principled dissent and destructive rebellion can be thin, and it is imperative to tread carefully.

Additionally, the choice to resist is often fraught with personal risk. It can lead to social ostracism, economic hardship, and even physical violence. Whistleblowers, for example, often face severe consequences for exposing corruption or wrongdoing within organizations. They may lose their jobs, face legal challenges, and suffer damage to their reputations. Yet, they choose to speak out, motivated by a sense of moral obligation to protect the public interest. The alternative – to remain silent and complicit in the face of injustice – is a far greater betrayal of one's own conscience. As Vaclav Havel, the dissident playwright and later president of Czechoslovakia, argued, living in truth, even under oppressive conditions, is a powerful act of resistance. It undermines the legitimacy of the system and inspires others to question the status quo. This "living in truth" can manifest in small, everyday acts of defiance, such as refusing to participate in propaganda, supporting marginalized communities, or simply speaking out against injustice when one witnesses it.

Moreover, it is important to acknowledge that resistance is not always a grand, dramatic gesture. It can be a quiet, persistent, and often unseen effort to challenge injustice from within. Think of the activists working tirelessly within bureaucratic systems to advocate for policy changes, or the teachers who subtly challenge oppressive curricula to empower their students. These forms of resistance, while less visible, can be just as effective in creating lasting change. They require patience, perseverance, and a deep understanding of the systems they are trying to transform.

The concept of "sanity" itself is subjective and culturally constructed. What is considered normal or acceptable in one society may be deemed deviant or even insane in another. Throughout history, those who challenged prevailing social norms have often been labeled as mentally unstable, as a way to discredit their ideas and maintain social control. Therefore, embracing the label of "lunatic" can be a form of empowerment, a way to reclaim the narrative and challenge the very definition of sanity. It is a recognition that true progress often requires challenging the status quo and questioning deeply ingrained assumptions.

We must understand that the sanity of resistance lies in its unwavering commitment to moral principles, even when those principles are unpopular or dangerous. It is about choosing dignity over conformity, truth over acquiescence, and freedom over fear. While the label of "lunatic" may be used to discredit and silence dissent, it should be embraced as a badge of honor by those who dare to challenge injustice and strive for a better world. For it is in the courage of these "lunatics," these dissenting voices, that the hope for a more just and equitable future resides. Their resistance, however unconventional it may seem, is not a sign of madness, but a testament to the enduring power of the human spirit to stand against oppression and fight for what is right. They remind us that true sanity lies not in conforming to a flawed system, but in striving to create a more just and humane world, even if it means being labeled a "lunatic" along the way, understanding that such a label often signifies a commitment to a higher truth, a truth that transcends the limitations of the present and points toward a more just and equitable future for all. Resistance, therefore, is not merely an act of defiance; it is an act of creation, a conscious effort to shape a world that better reflects our shared values and aspirations.

The Unquenchable Flame
RESISTANCE, SANITY,
AND THE "LUNACY" OF HOPE

The human story is like a complex mosaic made of asymmetrical pieces of triumph and tragedy, progress and regression. Throughout history, oppressive systems have risen and fallen, threatening to extinguish the very spark of humanity. Yet, even in the face of unimaginable darkness, a flame has persisted, fueled by the courage of individuals who dared to question, to resist, and to dream of a better world. This chapter is not a lament for lost ideals, but an affirmation of that enduring flame, a call to action against the destructive forces that seek to smother it, and a celebration of the "lunatics" who refuse to let it die.

The essence of humanity lies in its capacity for empathy, reason, and creativity. Destructive political systems, however, often operate by systematically undermining these very qualities. They promote conformity over critical thinking, obedience over ethical judgment, and fear over compassion. They thrive on division, manipulating narratives to pit individuals against each other and consolidating power in the hands of a select few. In such environments, the flame of humanity flickers precariously, threatened by the suffocating weight of authoritarianism and the corrosive influence of propaganda.

I am urging us to embrace the role of "outsiders." This is not an endorsement of isolation, but a recognition that those who stand apart from the mainstream often possess a clearer perspective on the injustices that plague society. By resisting the pressure to conform, outsiders can maintain their critical faculties, challenge prevailing narratives, and offer alternative visions for the future. They are the sentinels who guard the flame of humanity, ensuring that it is not extinguished by the winds of political expediency.

Cultivating critical thinking skills is vital to preserving the flame. In an age of information overload and manufactured consent, the ability to discern truth from falsehood, to analyze arguments, and to question authority is more crucial than ever. Critical thinking empowers us to resist manipulation, to identify the underlying ideologies that drive destructive political systems, and to articulate our own values and principles. It is the oxygen that sustains the flame of reason, allowing it to illuminate the path towards a more just and equitable world.

Central to maintaining the flame is the act of "speaking truth to power." This requires courage, as it often entails challenging powerful institutions and risking personal safety. Yet, silence in the face of injustice is a form of complicity, a tacit endorsement of the status quo. By speaking out, even in the face of adversity, we can expose the lies and hypocrisy that underpin destructive political systems. We can inspire others to resist, to reclaim their voices, and to demand accountability from those who wield power.

Personally, I advocate for "dignity over conformity, courage over complacency, and the sanity of resistance over the madness of silence." This is a powerful articulation of the values that underpin the flame of humanity. Dignity requires us to respect ourselves and others, to uphold ethical principles, and to resist the degradation of our moral character. Courage empowers us to act in accordance with our values, even when faced with fear and uncertainty. And the sanity of resistance recognizes that the pursuit of justice is not a sign of madness, but a testament to our rationality and our commitment to a better world.

I believe that the resisters, the truth-seekers, the dissenters, are the "lunatics" who can save the world. This is not a literal endorsement of insanity, but a recognition that unconventional thinking, a willingness to challenge the established order, and an untiring commitment to justice are often perceived as irrational by those who benefit from the status quo. It is precisely this "lunacy" - this refusal to accept the world as it is, this unwavering belief in the possibility of a better future - that fuels the flame of humanity and propels us towards progress.

We must not forget that the flame of humanity is not a passive entity; it is a dynamic force that requires constant tending and protection. It is fueled by our commitment to critical thinking, our courage to speak truth to power, and our willingness to resist the destructive forces that threaten to extinguish it. By embracing our role as outsiders, by cultivating these essential qualities, and by choosing dignity, courage, and the sanity of resistance, we can ensure that the flame of humanity continues to burn brightly, guiding us towards a future where justice, equality, and compassion prevail. Let us, therefore, embrace our "lunacy" and strive to be the saviors the world so desperately needs.

THE VITAL SPARK

DISSENT, RESISTANCE, AND ACTIVISM
As Guardians Of Democracy, Freedom, And Human Rights

Democracy, freedom, and human rights are not static achievements, gifted once and for all. They are fragile, constantly in need of nurturing and defense. When these cornerstones of a just society are threatened, dissent, resistance, and activism become not merely options, but vital necessities. They serve as the canary in the coal mine, alerting us to impending dangers and providing the necessary impetus to reclaim and revitalize the principles that underpin a free and equitable world.

The importance of dissent stems from its inherent connection to the pursuit of truth. Democracy thrives on open dialogue and the free exchange of ideas. When critical voices are silenced or suppressed, when narratives are controlled and dissent is demonized, the very foundation of informed decision-making crumbles. Dissent compels us to question established norms, scrutinize power structures, and consider alternative perspectives. It challenges the status quo, preventing complacency and fostering a climate of intellectual honesty, crucial for identifying and addressing the threats to our freedoms. Historically, marginalized communities have often been at the forefront of dissenting voices, highlighting injustices and challenging discriminatory practices that would otherwise remain hidden beneath the veneer of normalcy. Their dissent forces a reckoning with uncomfortable truths and paves the way for progress.

Resistance, in its various forms, is the active embodiment of dissent. It moves beyond mere expression of disagreement and translates it into concrete action. From peaceful protests and civil disobedience to organized campaigns and legal challenges, resistance challenges the legitimacy of unjust laws and policies. It represents the collective refusal to accept oppression and the determination to safeguard fundamental rights. When democratic processes are circumvented or manipulated, resistance becomes a crucial mechanism for holding power accountable. It reminds those in authority that their power is derived from the people and is contingent upon their adherence to the principles of justice and fairness. Without resistance, authoritarian tendencies can quickly take root, eroding democratic institutions and undermining the very freedoms they are meant to protect.

Activism, encompassing both dissent and resistance, provides the sustained and organized effort required to achieve meaningful change. It involves mobilizing communities, raising awareness, and advocating for specific policy changes. Activism transforms individual concerns into collective power, enabling marginalized groups to amplify their voices and demand redress. It leverages the power of information, education, and strategic action to challenge oppressive systems and promote social justice. When freedom of expression is curtailed, activists find creative ways to circumvent censorship and disseminate information. When human rights are violated, activists document abuses, pressure governments, and seek international intervention. Their tireless efforts ensure that the principles of democracy, freedom, and human rights remain at the forefront of political discourse and continue to inspire action.

The suppression of dissent, resistance, and activism is a hallmark of authoritarian regimes. It is a calculated strategy to silence opposition, maintain control, and perpetuate injustice. History is replete with examples of societies that descended into tyranny after silencing dissenting voices and crushing resistance movements. Conversely, periods of significant social and political progress have been marked by vibrant dissent, organized resistance, and active citizen engagement. The Civil Rights movement in the United States, the anti-apartheid struggle in South Africa, and the Arab Spring uprisings all demonstrate the transformative power of collective action in the face of oppression.

In conclusion, dissent, resistance, and activism are not merely abstract concepts. They are the vital spark that ignites the fight for justice, the bulwark against tyranny, and the driving force behind social progress. When democracy, freedom, and human rights are at risk, these practices become imperative for safeguarding the very foundations of a just and equitable society. They require courage, determination, and an unwavering commitment to the principles of human dignity and equality. As citizens of the world, we have a moral obligation to defend these practices and to support those who dare to speak truth to power, resist injustice, and actively work towards a more just and free world for all.

NEVER UNDERESTIMATE THE POWER YOU HAVE AS AN INDIVIDUAL AND AS A CITIZEN!

MORAL COURAGE IN A CORRUPT WORLD

The very definition of "sanity" is often presented as a neutral measure, a yardstick against which individual behavior is objectively assessed. However, a closer examination reveals that this yardstick is frequently held by those in power, its calibrations shaped by the prevailing political and social structures. In a corrupt system, what is deemed "normal" or "acceptable" becomes inextricably linked to the perpetuation of that corruption. In the following I am trying to grapple with the idea that in such environment, conformity is often a form of complicity, that the price of silence in the face of injustice is far too high, and that dissent, even when deemed "lunatic" by the established order, becomes not only a right but a civic duty. It underscores the critical role of moral courage in challenging oppressive power structures, even at the expense of social acceptance.

The notion that sanity is circumstantial hinges on the understanding that power structures define the boundaries of acceptable behavior. In a society riddled with corruption, those who benefit from the system naturally seek to maintain the status quo. This involves normalizing behaviors that uphold their power, and conversely, pathologizing behaviors that threaten it. Conformity, then, becomes a mechanism for ensuring the system's survival. To participate in the rituals of a corrupt system, to remain silent about its injustices, to passively accept its warped logic, is to actively contribute to its endurance. Therefore, "sanity" in such a context becomes synonymous with complicity.

The dangerous effect of this imposed sanity leads to the challenging problem of silence. The fear of reprisal, the desire for social acceptance, or the simple inertia of everyday life can all contribute to a collective silence in the face of injustice. However, the price of this silence is ultimately far too high. It allows tyranny to take root and flourish, enabling the unchecked abuse of power and the erosion of fundamental rights. By remaining silent, individuals become tacit accomplices in the very injustices they may secretly abhor. This silence not only empowers the corrupt but also perpetuates a cycle of fear, where dissenting voices are increasingly isolated and marginalized.

Against this backdrop, dissent emerges as a critical civic duty. Vigilant citizenship demands actively challenging abuses of power, even when such challenges come at a personal cost. This is not merely an abstract philosophical principle; it is a practical necessity for the preservation of a just society. Dissent can take many forms, from peaceful protest and investigative journalism to acts of civil disobedience and artistic expression. Regardless of its form, dissent serves as a crucial check on power, exposing corruption, holding leaders accountable, and fostering a culture of critical thinking.

What I want you to remember in any circumstances is that the "lunatic," the individual who dares to speak truth to power, can be a catalyst for positive change. Labeled as crazy, irrational, or even dangerous by the ruling elite and their apologists, these individuals often possess the moral clarity and courage to disrupt the status quo. By speaking out against injustice, they inspire others to question authority, awakening a sense of civic responsibility and prompting a re-evaluation of societal norms. Their "lunacy," in reality, is often a profound sanity, a refusal to accept the distorted reality imposed by a corrupt system. History is replete with examples of individuals initially dismissed as radical or insane who ultimately paved the way for significant social and political reforms.

Also, I have the strong belief that moral courage must ultimately trump social acceptance within an unjust system. Staying true to one's values is more important than fitting in or being liked by those who uphold corruption. This requires a steadfast commitment to principles of justice, fairness, and equality, even in the face of overwhelming pressure to conform. It demands the willingness to endure ridicule, ostracism, and potentially even persecution, for the sake of a greater good. This courage, born from a deep sense of personal integrity, is the bedrock upon which genuine social progress is built.

I do argue that the definition of "sanity" should be critically examined, particularly within the context of corrupt systems. When conformity becomes complicity, and silence empowers oppression, dissent becomes not just a right but a responsibility. The "lunatic" who dares to challenge the prevailing power structure can be a vital catalyst for change, inspiring others to question authority and fight for a more just world. Ultimately, it is crucial to understand the importance of moral courage, and I am urging individuals to prioritize their values over social acceptance and to actively resist the dangerous normalization of corruption. It is in this courageous dissent, in this perceived "lunacy," that the true sanity of a just and equitable society resides.

In a democratic society, the freedoms of speech, expression, and assembly are fundamental rights that enable citizens to participate in the political process and hold their leaders accountable. Dissent, resistance, and activism are crucial expressions of these freedoms, and are essential for the protection and preservation of democracy, freedom, and human rights.

Personally, I am deeply rooted in the principle that dissent is a fundamental right and a necessary practice. The act of expressing opposition or disagreement with the views or actions of the government or any other powerful institutions, is a vital component of a healthy democracy. It allows for the airing of different perspectives and the challenging of prevailing orthodoxies, which can lead to the development of new ideas and the improvement of policies. Dissent also serves as a check on the abuse of power, as it enables citizens to voice their concerns and hold those in power accountable for their actions.

In my perspective, resisting in the face of imminent danger is essential for our development, fostering critical thinking and analytical skills that drive progress. Resistance acts as a catalyst for evolution, pushing us to refine our thinking and advance as individuals and as a society. It can also take the form of awareness; and it should not be seen as an act of disobedience. The act of opposing or refusing to comply with policies or actions that are perceived to be unjust or harmful, is simply just another important form of political expression. Resistance can take many forms, from nonviolent protests and civil disobedience to more radical actions such as strikes and boycotts. Regardless of the form it takes, resistance is a powerful tool for bringing about change and protecting the rights and freedoms of individuals and communities.

Also, I believe that activism, or the use of direct action to bring about social or political change, is a critical component of a vibrant and functioning democracy. Activists work to raise awareness of important issues, mobilize public opinion, and advocate for policies that protect the rights and freedoms of all citizens. They are often at the forefront of efforts to challenge inequality, discrimination, and injustice, and their work is essential for the maintenance of a fair and inclusive society.

In order to build an inclusive, ethical, just and effective society we must understand that when democracy, freedom, and human rights are at risk, dissent, resistance, and activism become even more important. By speaking out against injustice, opposing repressive policies, and working to bring about positive change, citizens can play a critical role in defending their rights and protecting the democratic process. And as I said before, dissent, resistance, and activism are essential when democracy, freedom, and human rights are at risk. These forms of political expression allow citizens to participate in the political process, hold those in power accountable, and bring about positive change. By defending and exercising these rights, citizens can help to safeguard the future of democracy and protect the freedoms and rights of all individuals.

HOW "LUNATICS"
Change the World
THROUGH COURAGE
AND CRITICAL THOUGHT

History is besieged with the remains of discarded orthodoxies, the remnants of ideas once considered sacrosanct but now relegated to the dustbin of intellectual progress. Standing amidst these ruins are the figures who dared to challenge the established order, the "lunatics" whose pronouncements were initially met with scorn, derision, and even persecution. They were dismissed as madmen, heretics, or simply misguided fools, yet their unwavering commitment to their beliefs, coupled with the power of critical thought, ultimately vindicated them, transforming the world in the process. This essay will explore the history of these individuals, delving into the psychology of dissent that fueled their actions and offering practical strategies for finding one's own voice in the face of injustice.

From the ancient world to the modern era, the label of "lunatic" has been a powerful tool for silencing dissent. Socrates, the father of Western philosophy, stands as a potent early example. In 399 BC, the Athenian court condemned him, not for outright treason, but for "corrupting the youth" and "impiety" - accusations veiled in concerns about his relentless questioning of authority and traditional beliefs. His commitment to truth, even when it challenged the deeply held convictions of Athenian society regarding gods and the ideal state, led to his tragic execution by hemlock poisoning. Yet, his legacy endures, his Socratic method serving as a cornerstone of critical thinking and intellectual discourse, influencing philosophical inquiry for millennia. His insistence on "knowing thyself" and questioning everything cemented his place as a "gadfly" to the state, a role that ultimately cost him his life but secured his immortality.

Centuries later, Martin Luther, a relatively unknown Augustinian monk, ignited a religious revolution. In 1517, Luther, troubled by the sale of indulgences and other perceived corruptions within the Catholic Church, publicly posted his 95 theses on the door of the Wittenberg Castle Church. This act, seemingly small, was a direct challenge to the Pope's authority and the established religious order of Europe. He was branded a heretic, excommunicated by Pope Leo X, and threatened with death by the Holy Roman Emperor. Refusing to recant his beliefs, even when facing immense pressure and personal danger, Luther found protection among supportive German princes. His defiance, fueled by his conscience and a deep-seated belief in the individual's direct relationship with God through scripture, sparked the Protestant Reformation, a seismic shift in the religious and political landscape of Europe. Luther's willingness to stand alone against the established power structure irrevocably altered the course of history, leading to new Christian denominations and reshaping the political map of Europe.

The fight against slavery provides another compelling historical account of "lunatics" proving to be visionary. William Wilberforce, a British politician, dedicated his life to abolishing the slave trade in the British Empire. For decades, he tirelessly campaigned against the powerful lobbying forces of slave traders and plantation owners. He was ridiculed, ostracized by many of his peers, and his efforts were repeatedly thwarted. However, Wilberforce's unwavering moral conviction and his persistence in exposing the brutal realities of the slave trade eventually swayed public opinion and, after decades of struggle, led to the passage of the Slave Trade Act of 1807. His dedication to ending this inhumane practice, initially considered a radical and unrealistic goal, ultimately transformed British society and paved the way for the abolition of slavery itself.

In the 20th century, Mahatma Gandhi, a lawyer trained in London, employed non-violent resistance to challenge British colonial rule in India. His methods, which included peaceful protests, civil disobedience, and boycotts of British goods, were often met with violence and imprisonment. He was labeled a troublemaker, a fanatic, and a threat to the stability of the British Empire by many. Yet, Gandhi's unwavering commitment to non-violence and his ability to mobilize the Indian population ultimately forced the British government to grant India independence. He demonstrated the power of peaceful resistance in achieving political change, inspiring countless movements for civil rights and social justice around the world.

Similarly, Nelson Mandela was labelled a terrorist and imprisoned for 27 years for his fight against the apartheid regime in South Africa. He was considered a dangerous radical, a threat to the established order of racial segregation and white minority rule. The apartheid government sought to crush the African National Congress (ANC) and silence Mandela's voice. Yet, his unwavering commitment to equality and justice, his refusal to compromise on his principles, and his ability to maintain his dignity and moral authority even within the confines of prison ultimately led to the dismantling of apartheid and the birth of a democratic South Africa. Mandela's life stands as a testament to the power of perseverance and the transformative potential of standing against injustice, even in the face of overwhelming opposition and decades of imprisonment. He emerged from prison not as a broken man, but as a global icon of reconciliation and forgiveness.

These figures, and countless others like them, were not simply "crazy." They possessed a unique combination of courage, conviction, and critical thinking that allowed them to see beyond the accepted norms and envision a better future. Understanding the psychology of dissent is key to understanding their actions. At its core, dissent stems from a deep-seated moral compass, an intrinsic sense of what is right and wrong. It is driven by a rejection of injustice, a desire for a more equitable world, and a willingness to take risks to achieve that vision.

Speaking out against injustice is rarely easy. It often comes with significant challenges. Dissenters face social ostracization, professional repercussions, and even physical danger. The fear of these consequences can be paralyzing, preventing many from voicing their concerns. Yet, the rewards of speaking out can be profound. Beyond the potential for systemic change, dissent also offers a sense of personal integrity and the satisfaction of knowing that you have stood up for what you believe in. It empowers individuals to become agents of change, shaping the world around them rather than passively accepting the status quo.

So how can individuals cultivate the courage and critical thinking necessary to become effective dissenters? The first step is to develop strong critical thinking skills. This involves questioning assumptions, analyzing evidence, and considering different perspectives. Actively seeking out diverse sources of information is crucial in discerning fact from fiction and identifying biases. Rather than blindly accepting information, individuals must learn to dissect arguments, evaluate evidence, and draw their own conclusions. Practicing intellectual humility, the recognition that one's own understanding is limited and fallible, is also vital.

Finding your voice requires developing the ability to articulate your views effectively. This involves mastering the art of persuasive communication, learning to present your arguments in a clear, concise, and compelling manner. It also involves developing the emotional intelligence to engage in respectful dialogue, even with those who hold opposing viewpoints. Listening actively and empathetically to understand different perspectives, even when disagreeing, is crucial for effective communication and persuasion. Building a community of like-minded individuals can provide support and encouragement, helping to overcome the fear of isolation that often accompanies dissent. Mentorship from experienced activists and advocates can also provide invaluable guidance and support.

In conclusion, the history of "lunatics" who changed the world is a testament to the power of courage, conviction, and critical thought. These individuals, initially dismissed as crazy or misguided, ultimately reshaped society because they dared to challenge the established order. From Socrates questioning Athenian values to Mandela dismantling apartheid, their stories demonstrate the transformative potential of dissent. By understanding the psychology of dissent and developing the necessary skills to articulate our views effectively, we can all contribute to a more just and equitable world. The "lunatics" of history remind us that true progress often begins with the audacity to question the status quo and the unwavering commitment to speak truth to power. The sanity of dissent lies not in conforming to the accepted norms, but in striving for a better world, guided by reason, conscience, and the courage to challenge the injustice we see around us.

A CALL TO ACTION

BRIDGING ACROSS DIVIDES

The fight for freedom, as we've seen, requires more than simply resisting oppression; it necessitates actively building bridges across the chasms of division that weaken our collective strength. The battle against misinformation and the erosion of democratic values is not fought solely in the halls of power or on the pages of investigative reports; it's waged in the everyday conversations, the shared spaces, and the often-fraught interactions between individuals holding vastly different perspectives. The capacity for empathy, for active listening, and for identifying shared values—these are the crucial tools in our arsenal, just as important as a critical eye for biased reporting or a discerning ear for manipulative rhetoric.

The current political landscape, characterized by its extreme polarization and the echo chambers of social media, presents a formidable challenge. The ease with which individuals can curate their own informational diets, selecting only sources that confirm their pre-existing beliefs, fosters a climate of intellectual isolation and fuels animosity. This digital segregation limits exposure to dissenting viewpoints, hindering the ability to understand and appreciate diverse perspectives. Breaking through these echo chambers requires a conscious effort to engage with those who hold opposing views, to listen without judgment, and to search for areas of commonality, however small they may seem.

ACTIVE LISTENING One of the most effective strategies in bridging these divides is the practice of active listening. This isn't merely hearing what someone says; it's genuinely attempting to understand their perspective, their lived experiences, and the reasoning behind their beliefs. It involves setting aside preconceived notions and biases, suspending judgment, and approaching the conversation with a sincere desire to comprehend. Active listening necessitates asking clarifying questions, summarizing the other person's points to ensure understanding, and reflecting on the emotional undercurrents of the conversation. It demands patience, self-awareness, and a willingness to challenge one's own assumptions.

EMPATHY plays a crucial role in this process. Empathy is the ability to understand and share the feelings of another person, to step into their shoes and see the world from their perspective. It's not about agreeing with someone's viewpoint, but about recognizing the validity of their emotions and experiences. This requires acknowledging the human element in every interaction, recognizing that behind every political stance, every social belief, there lies a human story, shaped by unique circumstances and deeply held values. Cultivating empathy requires introspection and self-reflection, a willingness to acknowledge one's own biases and privileges, and a conscious effort to understand the lived realities of others.

FINDING COMMON GROUND, however seemingly elusive, is essential in fostering productive dialogue. While profound disagreements on fundamental issues may persist, there always exist areas of shared interest or values. Perhaps it's a shared concern for the well-being of children, a commitment to environmental protection, or a desire for a more just and equitable society. Focusing on these areas of commonality, however modest, can lay the foundation for constructive conversation and collaboration. It creates a sense of shared purpose and a platform for building trust and mutual respect.

STRATEGIES FOR PRODUCTIVE INTER-GROUP COMMUNICATION are crucial in bridging divides. These strategies extend beyond simply talking; they involve creating spaces for meaningful dialogue and interaction. Facilitated dialogues, utilizing trained mediators to guide discussions and ensure respectful communication, can be highly effective. These dialogues can involve structured exercises, such as shared storytelling or collaborative problem-solving, to encourage empathy and understanding.

COMMUNITY-BASED INITIATIVES play a pivotal role in this effort. Community gardens, neighborhood watch programs, and local volunteer organizations provide opportunities for people from diverse backgrounds to interact, collaborate, and build relationships. These shared experiences foster a sense of community, creating a more cohesive and understanding social fabric.

THE ROLE OF MEDIA cannot be overlooked. While media often exacerbates divisions, it can also play a vital role in bridging divides. Journalism committed to accurate reporting, fact-checking, and providing a platform for diverse voices can help counter misinformation and foster informed public discourse. Media outlets should actively seek to provide balanced coverage, presenting diverse perspectives and avoiding inflammatory language.

THE EDUCATIONAL SYSTEM has a critical role to play. Integrating empathy and intercultural understanding into curricula can equip future generations with the skills and knowledge to navigate a diverse and complex world. Education should not simply transmit information; it should cultivate critical thinking, emotional intelligence, and the ability to engage in productive dialogue with individuals holding diverse viewpoints.

The work of building bridges across divides is not a quick fix; it's a long-term commitment that requires sustained effort and unwavering dedication. It necessitates a conscious shift in mindset, a willingness to engage with those who hold opposing views, and a deep commitment to empathy, active listening, and finding common ground. It is a collective endeavor, requiring the participation of individuals, communities, and institutions alike. But the reward—a more just, equitable, and cohesive society—is well worth the effort. The alternative—a society fractured by division and animosity—is a path towards societal breakdown and the ultimate erosion of the freedoms we cherish. Building bridges is not simply an act of civility; it is a fundamental prerequisite for the preservation of democracy itself. It is a crucial component of our collective fight for freedom, a fight that extends far beyond the headlines and into the heart of our communities. This is a fight for the soul of our society, a battle for understanding, and a testament to the enduring power of human connection. The fight for freedom requires not only resisting oppression but also building bridges of understanding. This is a crucial aspect of reclaiming our freedoms and ensuring a future where diverse voices can be heard and respected. Only then can we truly secure the foundations of a just and free society.

A VISION
For a Better Future

The struggle for a more just and equitable future is not a solitary endeavor; it is a collective march toward a destination defined by shared values and mutual respect. While the challenges we face – the devious erosion of democratic norms, the corrosive influence of misinformation, and the pervasive inequalities that permeate our societies – are formidable, they are not insurmountable. The flame of hope, as flickering it may be at times, can be fanned into a roaring blaze through the concerted efforts of individuals committed to the pursuit of a better world.

This vision for a more just and equitable future is not an idealistic fantasy; it is a pragmatic roadmap built upon the foundations of established principles and demonstrable progress. It is a vision rooted in the belief that systemic change is achievable through persistent activism, strategic engagement, and the unwavering commitment to holding those in power accountable. It necessitates a profound shift in societal consciousness, a willingness to confront uncomfortable truths, and a dedication to building a more inclusive and participatory democracy.

One of the crucial pillars of this vision is the strengthening of democratic institutions. This requires more than simply preserving existing structures; it necessitates a fundamental overhaul of systems that have become corrupted or rendered ineffective by the relentless pursuit of power and profit. Reform of campaign finance laws, to eliminate the undue influence of money in politics, is paramount. Independent oversight of elections, ensuring transparency and accountability, is critical to maintaining the integrity of the democratic process. Judicial independence, safeguarding the rule of law and protecting vulnerable populations from abuse of power, is also vital.

The media landscape demands radical transformation. The proliferation of misinformation and disinformation, amplified by social media algorithms and partisan echo chambers, presents a grave threat to informed public discourse and rational decision-making. The need for independent, fact-based journalism that holds power to account is more urgent than ever. Supporting investigative journalism and promoting media literacy are essential in combating the tide of misinformation and fostering a more informed citizenry. Regulations are required to curtail the spread of falsehoods and ensure greater accountability for media outlets that engage in the dissemination of misinformation, without unduly restricting freedom of expression. A delicate balance must be struck between the protection of free speech and the imperative to safeguard against the spread of deliberate lies.

Education plays a pivotal role in cultivating the informed and engaged citizenry necessary for a flourishing democracy. Curricula must emphasize critical thinking, media literacy, and civic engagement. Students need to develop the skills necessary to navigate the complex information environment, to identify bias and misinformation, and to engage in constructive dialogue with those holding differing viewpoints. Equitable access to quality education, regardless of socioeconomic background or geographic location, is crucial to achieving this goal. The system needs to equip citizens with not only the knowledge but also the skills and confidence to participate fully and meaningfully in the democratic process.

The fight for economic justice is inextricably linked to the broader struggle for a more equitable future. Addressing systemic inequalities in wealth and income requires bold and transformative policies. Progressive taxation, aimed at reducing the concentration of wealth at the top, is essential. Investing in social programs that provide a safety net for vulnerable populations—including affordable healthcare, education, and housing—is critical to ensuring that everyone has the opportunity to thrive. Addressing the structural racism and other forms of discrimination that perpetuate economic inequality must be at the forefront of policy decisions. This requires not simply acknowledging these problems but actively dismantling the systems and structures that reproduce them.

Environmental sustainability is another crucial component of this vision. The climate crisis poses an existential threat, demanding immediate and concerted action. Transitioning to a green economy, investing in renewable energy, and adopting sustainable practices are not merely environmental concerns; they are essential for social and economic justice. A future where environmental concerns are ignored is a future characterized by immense inequality and instability, disproportionately affecting marginalized communities. The pursuit of environmental justice necessitates a fundamental restructuring of our relationship with the natural world, one that recognizes the interconnectedness of environmental, social, and economic well-being.

International cooperation is essential in addressing the global challenges that transcend national borders. Strengthening international institutions and fostering multilateral diplomacy are crucial in addressing climate change, promoting human rights, and preventing conflict. A commitment to international law and norms, coupled with a willingness to engage in constructive dialogue with other nations, is critical to building a more peaceful and just world order. The global community must work together to address shared problems and to build a more sustainable and equitable future for all.

The path toward a more just and equitable future is paved with challenges, but it is not a hopeless journey. The history of social movements demonstrates that collective action can bring about transformative change. The ongoing struggles for civil rights, women's suffrage, labor rights, and LGBTQ+ equality all bear testament to the power of people uniting to demand justice and reform. These successes, however hard-won, offer encouragement and provide a blueprint for future movements. They are a testament to human resilience, the power of collective action, and the capacity for positive social change.

The work ahead is immense, requiring firm commitment, persistent effort, and a refusal to succumb to despair. It calls for a renewed dedication to the ideals of democracy, equality, and justice. It demands a willingness to engage in difficult conversations, to confront uncomfortable truths, and to forge alliances across divides. The task of building a more just and equitable future requires the participation of everyone. It demands a fundamental shift in our understanding of our responsibilities to one another and to future generations. Only through collective action and relentless commitment can we hope to achieve this vision.

The vision for a more just and equitable future is a vision of hope. It is a belief in the capacity of humanity to overcome its challenges and build a better world for all. It is a reminder that the pursuit of justice and equality is not simply a moral imperative; it is a strategic necessity. This vision is more than a utopian dream; it is a necessary step forward for the survival and flourishing of both humanity and the planet. This vision, fueled by hope and a belief in our collective capacity for improvement, transcends mere moral aspiration and becomes a tactical imperative. A future governed by justice and equality is not simply desirable; it is the bedrock upon which sustainable societies, thriving economies, and a protected environment can be built. To abandon this pursuit is to condemn ourselves to a future rife with conflict, instability, and ultimately, decline.

Philosophically, the pursuit of justice and equity stems from a fundamental understanding of human dignity and inherent worth. To deny individuals their basic rights and opportunities based on factors like race, gender, socioeconomic status, or geographical location is to fundamentally devalue their humanity. This denial not only inflicts profound suffering on those directly affected but also undermines the potential for societal progress. When talent is stifled and voices are silenced, the collective creativity and innovation that drive advancement are diminished. Philosophers from Aristotle to Rawls have argued for the inherent injustice of unequal treatment, highlighting the corrosive effect of inequity on the social fabric. A society that embraces justice, on the other hand, creates an environment where individuals are empowered to reach their full potential, contributing to a richer and more dynamic society for all.

Politically, the quest for a just and equitable future requires a commitment to dismantling systemic inequalities and promoting inclusive governance. This involves challenging entrenched power structures, reforming discriminatory laws and policies, and ensuring that all citizens have equal access to resources, education, and opportunity. It demands a willingness to engage in difficult conversations about historical injustices and their lasting consequences, and to implement concrete measures to address them. Political institutions must be reformed to be more transparent, accountable, and representative of the diverse populations they serve. Furthermore, international cooperation is essential to address global inequalities, particularly in areas such as trade, climate change, and access to healthcare. The political landscape must shift from a focus on narrow self-interest to a broader understanding of the interconnectedness of societies and the imperative for collective action.

The argument that a just and equitable future is a strategic necessity rests on the understanding that inequality breeds instability and conflict. When vast disparities exist in wealth and opportunity, resentment and frustration fester, leading to social unrest and political polarization. This is evident in the rise of extremism, the proliferation of violence, and the erosion of trust in democratic institutions. Conversely, societies that prioritize justice and equity tend to be more stable, resilient, and prosperous. By investing in education, healthcare, and social safety nets, they create a more inclusive and cohesive society, where individuals are less likely to feel marginalized or disenfranchised.

The pursuit of this vision requires sustained effort, unstoppable dedication, and a steadfast belief in the power of collective action. It is a challenging path we must take, but the destination - **a world characterized by equity, fairness, and opportunity for all** - is a goal worthy of our unwavering commitment. The stakes are too high to fail. We must embrace the hopeful necessity of justice and equity, for the sake of ourselves, future generations, and the planet we call home.